Utopian Literature

Advisory Editor:
ARTHUR ORCUTT LEWIS, JR.
Professor of English
The Pennsylvania State University

The Art of Real Pleasure

Calvin Blanchard

Introduction by Arthur O. Lewis, Jr.

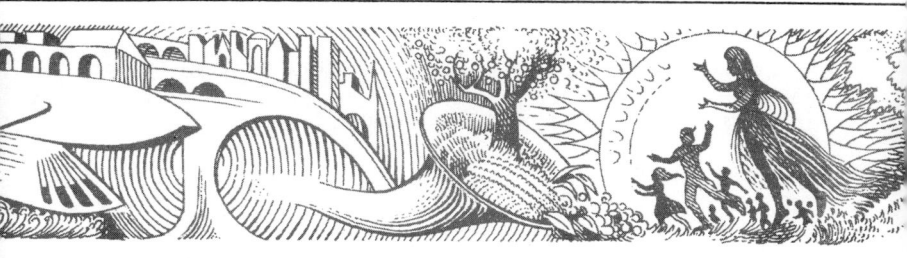

ARNO PRESS & THE NEW YORK TIMES
NEW YORK · 1971

Reprint Edition 1971 by Arno Press Inc.
Introduction Copyright 1971 by Arno Press Inc.

Reprinted from a copy in The Pennsylvania State University Library

LC# 70-154430
ISBN 0-405-03513-6

Utopian Literature
ISBN for complete set: 0-405-03510-1

Manufactured in the United States of America

Publisher's Note: This edition was reprinted from the best available copy

INTRODUCTION

IF THIS BOOK WERE TO ARRIVE BY MAIL, the recipient's first reaction might well be one of relief that it had arrived in a plain-brown wrapper. The very title page, *The Art of Real Pleasure: That New Pleasure for Which An Imperial Reward Was Offered* (anonymous too!), with Titian's Venus opposite as frontispiece, would surely increase that sense of relief. In any case for the nineteenth-century fantasizing adolescent or dirty old man (who else would have succumbed to the advertising and ordered the volume at eighty-five cents plus postage?) the new purchase would appear to justify his eager expectations. His delight would grow with the prefatory page which promises the reader that he will encounter more of these "ravishing beauties" in a "voluptuous feast" and with the next page where Lady Godiva faces a table of contents that lists still more "Pleasure That Is Pleasure," "Scenes We Would All Like To Be In," and "The Old Way And The New Way Spicily Contrasted." Turning idly through the book, "gay and gallant readers" would note for further more careful perusal a description of a night in what must surely be a high-class bordello, as well as retellings of "Putting the Devil Back in Hell" and similar tales from Boccaccio, Sachetti, and Margaret of Navarre. Continuing past the discussion of the necessity for legalizing free love as a bastion of society, the reader who continued to postpone immediate joys in favor of curiosity about later possibilities would find on the very last page an advertisement for his new treasure: "THE ART OF REAL PLEASURE is the most sensuous book ever written. It's the great secret revealed, of *perfect gratification, without troublesome consequences*. It's just what every man and every woman wants." Additionally there is another advertisement for the *Secret History of the Court of Charles the Second, including the Amours of the Duke of Buckingham and the Earl of Rochester*. Making a note to order this second delight for one dollar plus postage, the reader turns back to the first pages and begins the study of *The Art of Real Pleasure*.

But his anticipation is all wrong, for Calvin Blanchard was writing neither a companion volume to *Fanny Hill* nor a predecessor to Masters and Johnson. The "bordello" is only the Grand Saloon in the palace of the Grand Artist or chief leader of a wonderful new society, and the book itself is an interesting and significant description of what utopia might be like and how to attain it. For Blanchard, love unchained and science rightly used were to produce the "Glorious Panorama of Heaven on Earth."

Apparently his work had little impact in 1864 and has been virtually unknown since, but much of what Blanchard had to say could easily have been written a hundred years later. He is, in some minor respects at least, a kind of bridge between the technological society and the counter culture. Thus, for example, Blanchard describes the role of reason in human affairs: "Alas, for poor, impotent reason

... Reason does very little, except to choose between these and those circumstances, and try to acquiesce under them. It is instinct—desire—*passion*, that pushes ahead, whilst science and art clear the way." Theodore Roszak's view is not very different: "the decisive measure of the technology's essential criminality [is] the extent to which it insists, in the name of progress, in the name of reason, that the unthinkable become thinkable and the intolerable become tolerable" (*The Making of a Counter Culture*, 1964, p. 47). Blanchard explains the earlier failure of technology to produce a better world: "they who invented the machines and they who furnished the capital to put them into action attempted to run them for their own exclusive benefit." Herbert Marcuse writes in similar fashion when he says, "not technology, not technique, not the machine are the engines of repression, but the presence in them of the master who determines their number, their life span, their power, their place in life, and the need for them . . ." (*An Essay on Liberation*, 1969, p. 12). Finally it requires no great imagination to see Blanchard urging free love as a means to a society where war will be no longer necessary, by waving the student banner "Make Love Not War."

In any utopian writing, acknowledged or not (Blanchard's references to "Utopia" are sometimes derogatory), there are three essential parts: what is wrong with the present world, what the better world ought to be like, and how to get from the present to the better world. The parts are seldom well defined, and in the case of *The Art of Real*

Pleasure they are so intertwined as to be almost impossible to separate from each other. For Blanchard the present world was "the Dismal Ages" (sometimes "the Dark Age"), the better world was "the *Good Time*" (or "*Good Times*"), and the means of attainment was adoption of the principles of the "Religion and Government of Physical Science and Art," with implementation through the instrumentality of the Universal Mutual Guarantee Company. The Good Times are often described in terms of what they are not, and what they are not is frequently what the Dismal Ages had been; the means for achieving the Good Times are frequently part of the explanation of what the Good Times are.

Nevertheless, those aspects of the Dismal Ages that led Blanchard to propose his utopia are reasonably obvious. Nineteenth-century society was ugly in its environment, in its people, and in its ideas. It was full of mysticism and humbug, warfare and disease, jealousy and hypocrisy, pain and poverty, and, above all, "moral principle." This last was a kind of overall reason for the rest, the rationalization used to justify repression of the natural desires and goals of human beings. The foul-smelling old fogies recovered from the last quarter section of "old-worldishness" represent some of the evil this repression has produced. The six who survive the first day—four who die immediately are those who had enforced the old rules: soldier, constable, jailer, hangman—are minister, "red republican," professor of moral philosophy, politician, lawyer, and political economist. They prate of their own belief in duty and adherence to moral principle, but they are quickly informed that their world had really been one in which *duty*—more properly called *self-denial*—was nothing but an excuse, a kind of sour grapes attitude arising from ignorance of the means for self-gratification, leading to choices of only those goals which seemed achievable. Such choices led leaders to elect those paths which would bring them the most gratification, with consequent less fulfillment for the people as a whole. In the Good Time no such choices are necessary, and leaders have realized that they attain their own desires best through assuring that their followers attain theirs.

Blanchard's utopia has most of the material and spiritual benefits of the usual utopian society. Thus, "repulsive labor" is done by machines requiring a minimum of tending; all persons have opportunity to develop skills in which they can take pride. Exchange of goods is for the benefit of all and based on productivity rather than on artificially supported currency. Environment—both natural and man-made—is beautiful. Control of the atmosphere has brought an end to winter. The world is laid out into townships, each with a palace at the center in which the people dwell, "equal except in dimensions, to that wherein resides the Grand Artist." The education and upbringing of children are the business of the state. Marriage laws have been abolished and the relations between men and women made a matter of personal rather than public concern. Life is as long as one wishes to live, sickness is unknown, and death comes quietly when desired.

The social machine runs spontaneously, with leaders concerned with the welfare of all and social conditions established by the scientists and artists whose business it is to discover the best solutions to problems. Truly, as the motto of the Good Times puts it: "HUMANITY IS GOD: EARTH IS HEAVEN: LIBERTY IS REAL."

The means for bringing about the Good Times is, in Blanchard's view, a simple matter. It consists in permitting Nature to finish Creation, to complete man, "by creating all that his perfection, *as man*, requires." The corollary is recognition that "The sole business of government should be, not to repress, but *satisfy all human desire*. For mankind have *no* evil desires; they do but desire happiness; all the evil in the case arises from ignorance as to method." Contrastingly, in the Dismal Ages "to invent 'statutes' for crushing human nature out of men and women—has been the sole aim of government."

Although several minor suggestions are made for achieving utopia—for example, following the end of the Civil War, sell all war machinery and use the proceeds—the starting point, described variously at different points in the book, is "passing a law authorizing every man and every woman to *suit themselves in their love affairs*, and appropriating a sufficient sum to thoroughly educate all children, grammatically, arithmetically, geographically, and *physically*, and *provide* for them, so that they will *all* have *useful*, attractive, and sufficiently remunerative employment . . ." This basic law of the Religion and Government of Physical Science and Art will lead to the better world in which all mankind holds shares in the Universal Mutual Guarantee Company and is assured gratification of all its desires: "For self-interest, when rightly understood, will work as admirably as gravitation does, when we build, and operate in every respect, in accordance of a *thorough* knowledge of it."

The new system works because "*Nature, through art, has at length provided the means of following our own inclinations to the benefit instead of injury of each other.*" Stripped of the need to injure others for personal gain, because everyone can now have what he wants, the "women enchantingly beautiful" and the "men faultless" of this era can truly agree with the chief doctrine of the "Primary Catechism" to which the narrator and the six old fogies are introduced: that all human endeavor must aim at "the acquisition, perfection, and sufficient prolongation of happiness." The Catechism goes on to point out that "mankind . . . are now happily, a harmoniously organized whole . . ." so that any act which promotes individual happiness will promote that of collective mankind. Each individual is a part of the body politic, the functions of which the Catechism likens to those of the individual human body. As the individual body has nerves and brains, so too the body politic has "its Scientific Discoverers and Directors," through whom the individual exerts his will: "By means of these, I acquire the aid of the whole force of the body politic and of all else in the connection, and am thus enabled to shape my actions in accordance with the Social Organism's welfare, and simultaneously with the welfare of every part of it, necessarily including *myself*." Citizens of this new world are incapable of voluntarily striving for anything but what is right.

The specific means nature has provided is the increased population born into a world without the restrictions of marriage laws and social stigma. "Able bodied and able headed producers make all the wealth the world has, or can have." Hence all children must be "cared for as most precious acquisitions to the State." Adoption of these principles has brought about the Good Times in only three or four generations. Society has been able to "organize labor, capital, skill, and love affairs, *so that every man and every woman can act just as they naturally please* to act."

All this is so promising that one wonders—momentarily—about finding the twentieth century still a part of the Dismal Ages rather than of the Good Times; surely even Blanchard's shortsighted peers could see the merit of his proposals. But more sober reflection produces reason enough for our own sad state. In the first place, the book obviously had only minor effect, if any, on the society of 1864. And in the second place, the plan proposed, such as it is, is very incomplete.

The failure of the book to have any contemporary impact is easily understood. Blanchard made the serious mistake of writing a book meant for one kind of audience in a manner which appealed to a very different kind. The reader who bought the book in response to titillating advertisement would possibly read the whole book in hopes of getting his money's worth, but his disappointment at the tame entertainment and his frustration with the reforming zeal of the last pages would lead him no further. For him, "Love unchained" would be a cop-out. On the other hand, no serious social reformer would have bought the book to begin with, and if by chance it came into his hands, the first five minutes of reading would persuade him he had only a salacious and shallow volume before him. He would be unlikely to proceed beyond the first few pages and might indeed condemn the book to others. For him, "Love unchained" would be merely another excuse for promiscuity and social irresponsibility. Neither class of readers would be likely to attempt implementation of Blanchard's proposals.

The second reason for the failure of the book is that it offers only a cursory plan for achieving utopia. Blanchard's proposals have much in common with those of other utopian writers. He clearly believed that human nature is essentially good, that it is the destiny of man to mold the universe to his specifications, and that release of mankind from the inhibitions of traditional morality will lead to immediate betterment of society. He acknowledged Fourier, Comte, and Feuerbach, among others, as chief sources of his plan. In the garden of statues erected to those to whom the Good Times pays homage, these and other scientists and artists are recognized. There is little, however, beyond mere assertion to support the claim that Blanchard's reforms will be successful. Unlike many utopians he does not attempt to overwhelm his reader with statistics and tables of organization.

The final effect of enthusiastic assertion as opposed to carefully described plans is that the reader does not take the proposal seriously. Cries against war, poverty, disease, prostitution, dishonesty, tyranny, and other evils have been heard throughout the centuries of man's existence. Utopians have been suggesting panaceas for the ills of society for perhaps as long. But mere hatred of evil or anguish over human degradation or an idealistic view of human nature has never been enough to move society to change its unsatisfactory ways.

In the end men reject immediate cures and resume the slow climb toward what most of us hope will be a better life. At those times when the progress seems slower and the road steepest, it is easy to wish that fiction were reality and that the Calvin Blanchards of the world were proved right. And in a world where so often the future has the face of chaos we may be forgiven for wondering if the solution might not be to take that idealistic first step the Calvin Blanchards assure us will bring "the Good Times." Perhaps, we dream, tomorrow's mail will bring its new work, in plain brown wrapper, and this time it will hold the answer.

ARTHUR O. LEWIS
MAY 1971

THE ART

OF

REAL PLEASURE:

THAT

NEW PLEASURE,

FOR WHICH

AN IMPERIAL REWARD

WAS OFFERED.

NEW-YORK:
PUBLISHED BY CALVIN BLANCHARD;
"1864."

ENTERED, according to Act of Congress, in the year 1864, by Calvin Blanchard, in the Clerk's Office of the District Court of the United States, for the Southern District of New-York.

VENUS,

QUEEN OF LOVE AND BEAUTY.

As painted by Titian.

Is'nt she charming? Well, imagine her charms increased tenfold, and you will have some idea of the ravishing beauties to whom you are about to be introduced.

And if you can farther imagine these enchanting creatures, with perfect freedom in the embraces of lovers also without fault or blemish, and not the slightest disagreeableness in the case, either before or afterwards, you can get a foretaste of the voluptuous feast to which I have the high felicity to invite you.

Keep your imagination CLEAR, *and don't be afraid of raising it too high.*

LADY GODIVA

CONTENTS.

PART FIRST.
PLEASURE THAT IS PLEASURE—THE NEW MODE OF ENJOYMENT.

PART SECOND.
SCENES WE WOULD ALL LIKE TO BE IN.

PART THIRD.
THE OLD WAY AND THE NEW WAY SPICILY CONTRASTED.

THE ART

OF

REAL PLEASURE.

PART FIRST.

PLEASURE THAT **IS** PLEASURE.—THE **NEW MODE** OF ENJOYMENT.

My gay and gallant readers:
I am about to open for you a mine of pleasure, incomparably richer than you ever dared to hope this world of ours contained. I am going to uncover the long hidden fountain of *pure delight*, and point out *a way as easy as you can wish*, to secure the privelege of *bathing in that fountain to your entire satisfaction.*

Philosophers who have somehow or other secured a reputation for superior wisdom, tell us that life can, at best, be only a sort of half and half of pain and pleasure; that the happiest condition attainable is that of ease or comfort; a condition so wearisome that no man or woman of average feeling or intellect ever endured it without the aid of stimulants either spiritual or spirituous, or some other sort of deviltry. Now if this be so, what's the use of telling it? What's the use of philosophizing over it? What's the use of anything?

Evidently if this stale doctrine be true, any kind of fiction is better than truth and "the creator" has given us very queer proofs of "*His*" wisdom and goodness.

But it's not true. It is only the time-sanctioned nonsense of the grave and solemn fools who tag after old Granny Habit, and I undertake to upset the whole thing. I am going to exhibit, and minutely describe, *pure delight*—pleasure fully and completely satisfying to all the senses, with nothing unpleasant in the case; and I further undertake to show how that pleasure can be obtained. Mark this promise well, and hold me strictly to its fulfilment.

However strange and wonderful my description, or rather narrative shall appear, I promise not to go beyond the exact truth in any *essential particular*.

Read my book through, and then criticise it as severely as you please.

And now, without further preliminary, imagine yourself and myself in a palace (a *real* one, mind you, not a baseless "castle in the air") as much more splendid and agreeable than the Tuilleries or Windsor Castle, as you can *clearly* conceive. Don't be afraid of overdoing the picture; it's as much as the most brilliant intellect can do to come up to it.

The Grand Saloon of this palace is just comfortably filled with ladies and gentlemen. The ladies are all as beautiful as they could be, had almighty ingenuity and immaculate taste been exerted to the utmost in their creation; and all the gentlemen are as agreeable and every way as complete and perfect as though they had been made to the ladies' order.

The dresses of both ladies and gentlemen are of very light material, but richer and more beautiful than the finest tissues of India or Cachmere, and their fashion is perfectly graceful and easy.

The chief, or, Grand Artist, as he is entitled, enters, and exchanges salutes with the company.

We are not at a ball; we are only at an assembly, such as takes place every evening. But if we please to dance, as some of us generally do, we have only to touch a spring, and music, incomparably more rapturous than king or emperor ever heard, fills this magnificent hall; nor does the music come from cat-gut scrapers and brass-mouthing cheek-splitters; science has obviated all that.

Here I wish to draw particular attention to a friend of mine; a poet. As he has long been my companion, the glories we behold are not unexpected by him; still, he is not fully prepared for all their concomitants. He has written sonnets on "love-constancy," "family joys," and all that sort of thing. But he is now in a fair way to be converted to the doctrine of *universal* love, if for no other reason than his inability to choose between the ravishing beauties who, with the utmost freedom, entwine their arms around him, and me, and the other gentlemen, not omitting the Grand Artist himself. They ply us with glances from eyes so brilliant that we feel in a perfect glow of love; their attractions are so equal, that there is *absolutely* no difference in them; we would just as soon touch and take, as choose, with the *non-essential* and *mere passing* exception about to be named.

These beautiful houris permit us to encircle their fairy forms without the intervention of either iron or whalebone. They tempt us to snatch such ravishing kisses; we impress those kisses on their taper hands, their ivory necks, their honied lips, their voluptuous bosoms.

Their dancing is far more graceful than that of Taglioni or Elsler. Their voices are sweeter than the finest tones of the flute.

And jealousy is banished hence; here, as I have already said, there is no positive inferiority. If the dark-eyed brunette pleases us first, the azure-eyed blonde delights us next, and so on through the whole charming variety. And as the tastes of both ladies and gentlemen are equally varied, it comes right all round. We talk as sociably with our partners about our gallantries with others, as we dilate on the aroma of different roses, or the flavor of various wines and fruits.

Amid scenes like these, the hour for retirement steals on unawares. As the silver-toned bells chime that hour, evening zephyrs more balmy than ever wafted o'er Ceylon or Araby in times long passed, breathe through harp-strings of ravishing tone, sending soft love music through tasteful and elegant apartments, sacred to Venus's crowning joys, where perfect men and perfect women, in rapturous freedom, beget their kind, by night or by day, as they feel most inclination.

And now comes the grand excitement of the evening—taking partners for the night. All being equally loveable, the *style of beauty* that will please *our present taste* is the only question to be decided; and it happened now, as it generally does, that before half the party can make a selection, or get mated, the rest are so mutually and promiscuously enraptured with each other, as to be unable to tell which lady or gentleman charms them the most, and the question has to be decided by lottery.

Before the sweet sports began, I perceived that a blue-eyed houri had decided the choice of my friend the poet, and I knew beforehand, as the sequel will show, that he had decided her's. They were the first couple that retired.

As to myself, I was so absorbed in beholding and helping on the enjoyment of others, that I remained in the saloon till the lots were all drawn.

The nymph who fell to my share had hazle-brown eyes. Her ringlets fell over a neck and shoulders of matchless form and symmetry. Her breasts were of a charmingness surpassing all description, and so was every part of her; she was absolute perfection.

A glance in each other's eyes assured us that chance had been as kind to us as choice could have been—more kind, if anything; for there seemed to be additional piquancy in chance itself, where choice could have been founded only on a passing fancy.

Talk of love-constancy? there can be no such thing, till *each is constant to all, and all are constant to each.* Talk of the family tie? that tie will be either a galling fetter or a rope of sand, *till it includes the whole human family.* Say, or sing "There's no place like home?" there can be no place *like* home, *till there is no place* BUT *home in all the world.*

The apartment to which my charmer conducts me is of ample size, and perfectly ventillated. The ceiling presents the appearance of a canopy of flowers, wherein nestle Cupids, painted after models far more lovely than Grecian or Roman artist ever conceived. On the walls, Venus and her favorites are pictured to the life, as Goddesses and Gods do at length *really* exist; and we see them in all their charmingness, and in the most rapturous conditions. These apartments are sealed to all who have not attained to ripe puberty; the example of parents *does not now introduce mere children to withering prematurity.*

At one end of our chamber, pure water sparkles in chrystal baths; our bed occupies the centre. It is of elastic, spungy material, filled with air, which we can change at pleasure. It has a small, peculiar under covering spread in the center for a special purpose; and across its foot-rail hang sheets of finest linen—the only upper covering that is ever needed. Its *toute ensemble* is so arranged and coloured, that it presents the appearance of a bed of roses; and she who now, in most exquisite gracefulness, reclines thereon, is incomparably sweeter than all the roses in the universe.

A cushion of the finest velvet sustains her lovely form at an angle that displays all her charms, leaving nothing to be desired but their enjoyment.

When I devote myself to love, I also devote myself to worship; with me, love is inseparable from adoration; woman is my *beau ideal* of perfection.

I kneel to my divinity; I kiss her feet, with a fervency no saint ever felt, except, perhaps, approximately, while in ecstasies before the *Virgin's* shrine.

Oh, how women love to be worshipped; it's a positive necessity of their nature; it's at the bottom of what is so ill-temperedly censured as coquetry. Tyranny has made kneeling the attitude of debasement; but there can be no debasement in kneeling to the concentrate incarnation of all that is adorable —to woman; the bravest heroes and wisest men the world has ever seen, have been woman worshippers.

My Goddess presents her hand; she offers it so naively; she displays it so *artistically artless*. I press that fairy hand in both my own, and cover it with kisses. Then, in an ecstasy, I clasp her in my arms, and drink delicious nectar from her ruby lips.

Her ivory neck and shoulders next receive my kisses; but I shower them most profusely, and press them longest, on her fragrant bosom; whilst my ardent hands rove instinctively to where love most powerfully invites—to the very fountain of life and bliss, overflowing with quintessent amour.

Into that pure fountain, love's ready agent—nature's most wonderful instrumentality eagerly plunges; now we feel the unspeakable raptures of love's glorious consummation; now we know what enchantment *really is*. But description can give only a very faint idea of the exquisite bliss of love's crowning act with this enchanting creature; its thrill through every nerve and sinew; its voluptuous prolongation; its ecstatic reciprocalness.

She is just in the right condition for loving; so am I. All-powerful Nature irresistibly invites to it. Our passions, completely unshackled, and unprovoked either by *opposition*, or *abnormal stimulation*, sweetly urge us on ; we *freely* give ourselves up to pleasure's full sway ; we revel in such *pure* delight, as can alone beget human beings worthy their high name, and an honour to their exalted nature.

We achieve love's critical acme both together. Our ecstasies are simultaneous, full, and mutual. Our whole being is wrought up to such blissfulness as the most fortunate voluptuaries of past ages experienced only a slight approximation to.

After the grateful refreshment of the bath, we resign ourselves to sleep in each others arms, our hearts in happiest accord with *The Great Universal Heart*, and glowing with unfeigned admiration for *The Real Omnipotency*, wherein we " live, move, and have our being;" wherein we completely achieve our happiness, and spontaneously do our part in accomplishing the glorious end and aim of all existence.

PART SECOND.

SCENES WE WOULD ALL LIKE TO BE IN.

But I must hasten to tell you about my friend the poet; what he experienced this happy night.

We met early next morning, among the fairy bowers. His countenance was one radiant sparkle of joy, with just the least possible tinge of shame; just enough to tell that his philosophy had proved a failure, and he had made up his mind to confess it.

I told him of my loves, and he told me of his. But when he came to the end of the consummation of his joys, he broke off so queerly that I suspected something which he wished to keep back had happened, and so expressed myself.

"Come, my friend," said I, "out with it. I have confessed many mistakes, and I assure you that, however much it mortified me to do so, I felt a great deal better for it afterwards."

This gave him courage.

"Well," said he, "after I had taken the bath, which, by the by, had such an exhilirating effect that I felt almost as gallant as at first, I said to my charmer in a tone that probably smacked a little of jealousy—' To-morrow night, my love, I suppose you will be as happy in the arms of another as you have just now been in mine.'"

"'Not quite so soon as that,' she replied. "'At least I don't feel just now as though I should. But this is the worst possible time to decide the question. Whenever nature does again prompt me to the love-play, she will probably tempt me to change partners, judging from former experiences. My dear friend, I love variety in nothing so much as in love; and such is the taste of a very large majority of people; probably of all. There are a few who profess constancy, as they call it; but whether they practice it or not, nobody takes the trouble to inquire. Perhaps you are one of the constants. If so, I will to-morrow introduce you to a lady of that profession, who looks for all the world just like me. Do you think she will content you?'

"'For life! for ever!' I exclaimed.

"'Meanwhile,' she continued, 'there are two couches in our apartment. On this one I shall repose. Behind yon curtain you will find another, provided for just such accidents as seem to have happened here to-night. Choose in which of these beds you will dream of your partner for life.'

"And so you sneaked away to the lonely couch behind the curtain, I suppose," said I; "I don't wonder you feel ashamed to confess it."

"No, my friend," said he, "without a moment's hesitation, I chose the bed whereon she had already reclined with a grace that would have tempted a saint from "Paradise" if he had a spark of manhood remaining. But just out of curiosity, I took a peep behind the curtain at the other bed. From all appearances, it had never been tumbled, and I don't believe it ever will be."

"It's probably tumbled out of the room before now," said I, " for it was placed there at my suggestion, expressly for the purpose it has so happily served. But here comes the lady, who will give you all further information you may need in the matter, and she is attended by another who appears to be her second self. It's your 'partner for life,' I'll be bound. I wish you joy, my dear friend. Good morning."

When the fashionables come to buy this book, I hope they will not light on this part of it. What! ladies and gentlemen taking the air before sunrise, the morning after a *soiree?* The gentlemen will be expected to yawn and stretch in bed, and complain of the headache till 11 o'clock at the earliest; and then crawl languidly forth to enquire of the servant or the family doctor how Miss or Mrs. feels after their fatigues; and it will be considered 'positively vulgaw' for a lady to get over those fatigues without a day's nursing, and a dose of rhubarb and magnesia, or a seidlitz powder at the very least.

But I have a world of wonders to relate, and cannot dwell longer on this one just now. I promise to make all clear, however, before I have done.

The palace I have already described is only one —the largest one—that helps to compose the City of Palaces—the Capitol of the world. The world itself is laid off into townships, in the centre of each of which there is a palace, inhabited by *the people,* equal except in dimensions, to that wherein resides the Grand Artist or his assistants. There is not in the whole world a single private or isolated residence, not one of those narrow abodes of jealousy and *ennui,* wherein people used to pray, and swear, and fret themselves to death " *all for the best.*"

All labor that is in the slightest degree repulsive is done by machinery. Motors far more effective than steam, and unattended by anything disagreeable, are in perfectly successful operation.

Science and art have stilled tempests, quelled volcanoes, sufficiently equillibriated thermal action between the equator and the poles, and sufficiently introduced luminous action at the latter.

All the marshes and deserts are in a state of high cultivation. The atmosphere is everywhere perfectly salubrious. Sickness is no more. Death itself is *practically* abolished. Everybody lives as long as they want to ; they live till repetition wears out all conceivable variety, and then resign themselves to everlasting forgetfulness with as little pain and regret as they go to sleep every night.

Now, don't pronounce this impossible. If you do, you will make as big fools of yourselves as did the Esquimaux on being told that such places as Paris, London, and New York existed; and that steamboats, railroads, and telegraphs were in successful ooperation. I tell you that electro-magnetism and kindred science had scarcely begun to be developed in the nineteenth century.

But here comes a messenger, not a servant, but a sylph, as beautiful as any to whom I have introduced you.

"His Highness, the Grand Artist, will reserve a seat for you beside him at breakfast."

Behold me seated at the table, next to the ruler of the world.

Such a breakfast—one that so delighted the taste and suited digestion, you, reader, never sat down to; the best hotels now furnish no meals at all comparable to it. The bread, the wine, the fruits, the vegetables, and the *cookery*, were exactly what the highest science and art had decided were calculated to give life just the desirable length, and qualify it for being desirable. Meat furnished no part of the repast, and I hardly need to add, that all the ladies and gentlemen freely helped themselves without the annoyance of waiters.

After breakfast, the Grand Artist said to me, "My friend, I am going to tell you something that is a great puzzle to us. Perfection does not yet reign quite everywhere; there is one little plague-spot, a *very* little one, only an old-fashioned 'quarter section,' wherein it seems as though all the old-worldishness is concentrated. The horrible stink of the place prevents ingress, whether by land or air; and it is enveloped in a mist too thick for the sharpest eye-sight, aided by the strongest glasses, to penetrate."

"Will your Highness consign this 'quarter section' nuisance to my control?" I asked.

"Most willingly;" was the response.

"Where is it? I will take the management of it instantly."

"We will show you the spot, and second you in your undertaking," replied twenty voices at once.

We started right off, and were within smelling distance of the place in less than an hour. Its stench was indeed terrible even to myself, who had only quite recently become unused to it; of course, it was intolerable to my companions, none of whom had ever experienced more than its slightest sniff. It was what the most austere saints of the "Dark Ages" called the "odour of sanctity." People generated and kept it up by neglecting and abusing their corporeity for the supposed benefit of their "mentality," or "souls." It smelt like the suds in which the chemise of *honest* old maids and old bachelors had been washed. It was the effluvia of humanity's life principle, putrified through deprivation from use. You, reader, constantly smell it more or less, but habit has made it "second nature," and so you do'nt mind it, unless you happen to be so uncommonly sensitive and nice as to be considered "cynical," or at least "odd."

Before starting, I had provided myself with a large flask of whiskey, of which I now took a good swig, and invited my companions to do the same.

"We can't drink this horrid stuff," said they, "it's only used in chemistry."

"Down with it," said I, "unless you mean to back out of your undertaking. Our forefathers very often had recourse to a much worse article than this. It did them a great deal of harm, but more good. A night's drunkenness, even when it came to that, was far better for their health than a night of sleepless sorrowing. It was an excellent guardian against malaria, and just the thing for a very trying emergency."

After we had drunk ourselves into that condition in which we would have assaulted the "Devil" himself, we made a rush for the centre of the infernal "quarter section."

"There's the core of this nasty ulcer," said I, pointing to ten strange looking creatures, huddled together in a very narrow concern: and we seized and dragged them out, in little more time than it has taken to write it. At first, we thought they were stone dead; but a close examination showed that they were only very fast asleep.

Our dash into the place was followed by a current of the pure surrounding air, and the change was immediately and most agreeably perceptible. In ten minutes, the foggyness had wholly disappeared, and very little of the old fashioned scent remained, except on the strange creatures, and a plentiful shower of perfumery soon made them endurable.

To guard against contagion, some of our party who had kept to the windward, suggested the plan of fumigating the creatures with tobacco—an article which, like whiskey, was still used in chemistry. This suggestion created roars of laughter; for at the distance of half a mile to the leeward it was unmistakably evident that they were but too well saturated with that abomination.

We telegraphed the news of our success to the Capitol, and the Grand Artist despatched a corps of engineers, whose ingenious and powerful machinery took the creatures we had found, together with the concern in which we found them, to the City of Palaces.

And what, reader, do you suppose that concern was? It was neither more nor less than an old fashioned "homestead." It was such a house as people lived in at the epoch of "civilization," who did not occupy a still more uncomfortable one in some crowded, dirty, plague-breeding city. It was a fair sample of the "sweet homes" wherein people prayed, and swore, and fretted themselves to death, whilst breeding slaves, knaves, skin-flints, hypocrites, and fools, and multiplying victims for war, pestilence, famine, the alms house, the brothel, the prison, and the gallows.

Our entry into the City of Palaces was a perfect triumph. The sky was almost darkened, by balloons, with their cars full of ladies and gentlemen, *really* divine—anxious to get a sight at our trophy.— Never before since the Good Time set in, had curiosity been at so high a pitch, enthusiasm so great, excitement so intense. The scene was magnificent beyond description.

The creatures we had discovered resembled the human beings that had at length been created about as nearly as the "What Is It?" resembled the people who used to pay Barnum their quarters for a look at it. Their toggery was as inconvenient and uncomfortable as possible, and seemed chiefly intended to increase their ugliness. Curiosity prompted certain of the bystanders to strip it off, and the most laughable mistakes were made in putting it on again; it was next to impossible to get the hang of it.

The savans, to whose further examination we committed these singular creatures, decided that they were human beings of a very ancient type, and undoubtedly belonged to that class which the extreme radicals (those who had *some* foresight of *real* progress) characterised as "old fogies." The proofs seemed to show that they had bemuddled their brains over social fossilization till they had, through constant sympathy with their own morbidness, attained the most complete, sound, and orthodox state of petrifaction that admitted of *any life at all ;* in which condition nature, by one of her strange freaks, had, as if to punish their obstinacy, fixed them.

In the pocket of No. 1 was found a receipt in full for a year's preaching, and a sermon in favour of total depravity, original sin, and all but universal damnation. It didn't take much fumbling among old records to prove him an "orthodox parson."

The pockets of No. 2 were crammed with printed debates; a fair sample of which was one as to whether "God" ever made any special communication to a certain very ancient individual named "Moses." A pamphlet was also found on this fellow, containing a vast quantity of reason and argument, going to show that people would be as well off as they are capable of becoming, if they would generally disbelieve "The Bible," turn the "gospel shops" into common school houses, stick to gold, silver, and copper money; divide the world into 60-acre lots, or "quarter sections," to be owned exclusively by cultivators, keep the game of caucus and ballot-box or "rotation in office" in full play, and either get married or get along somehow without sexual gratification. No. 2 was evidently an out and out "infidel" of the dryest kind—a thorough "red republican."

That No. 3 was a professor of "moral philosophy" was quickly decided. On his person were found a well-read volume entitled "The Riches of Poverty and Benefits of Affliction," and the millionth treatise to prove that if everybody would subdue their most vehement natural passions, "do as they would be done by," and "be content with little," (with about a thousandth part of what they instinctively crave) the height of earthly perfection would be attained.

No. 4 had a ring on his finger with the initials S. A. D. On this abominable creature were found notes of a stump speech, showing in most bunkum rhetoric, that "the price of freedom is eternal vigilance," that "the tree of liberty must be ever and anon watered with human blood;" that "*majority rule is the utmost possible freedom and the highest law;*" that in accordance with this liberty and this law, "the weaker have no rights which the stronger are bound to respect;" and finally that majorityism is "the noblest system of government ever devised by mortals," or devisable by them.

No. 5 had a single piece of evidence as to his profession, but that was conclusive. It consisted in a law decision, that the good of society requires a woman to remain the wife of a husband who beats her every day with a cudgel "no thicker than his thumb," gets constantly drunk on her earnings, and whips his and her children into the street to beg, steal, go to the poor-house, or minister to a certain unmentionable depravity to which grave and reverend debauchees were principally addicted, till they became old enough for pimps or prostitutes.

There was sufficient evidence on No. 6 to prove him a political economist, who contended that "marriage" in accordance with the foregoing law decision was the great safeguard from licentiousness, and the best possible guaranty for the rights of women and children ; and that, but for the constraint on sexual freedom which such marriage imposed, the world would soon be overpopulated.

"Is it possible," exclaimed several of the company, their angelic countenances pale with horror, "that the people from which we are descended were ever subjected to such politicians, such lawyers, such moralists, and such religionists ?"

"Yes," replied I, "the thing is but too painfully evident."

"But how could such infernalism be enforced ? Surely, it could not be *spontanized*, like *our* system," remarked a ravishing beauty who evidently spoke the feelings of all the other ladies present.

"Let us continue the examination," said I, " and see if we cannot solve the question by that means."

Nos. 7, 8, 9, and 10 proved to be *a soldier, a constable, a jailer, and a hangman.*

Scarcely had the examination been completed when the four last subjects of it went into convulsions and died ; their constitutions were too abnormal to endure such a sudden introduction to pure surroundings.

To preserve the six remaining old fogies from a similar fate, we crammed their mouths full of the strongest tobacco we had, filled their noses with some of it powdered into " snuff," placed them back in their homestead, burnt a lot of brimstone therein, and tightly closed the doors and windows.

These strange creatures, and the adventure of

myself and companions in bringing them to light, were the all-absorbing topic; supper was almost neglected; and the usual *soiree* dwindled to little more than a conversation club.

But the enchanting game of partners for the night was not omitted. I caught a glimpse of my poetic friend with his arm very close around the waist of the lady he had fallen so vehemently in love with from description, and simultaneously perceived that the beautiful creature he had spent his first love night with, was trying her most bewitching seductions on me. As nothing could suit me better, I hastened to reciprocate her advances, remarking, in order that she might not be disappointed in any part of her expectations, that her amiable companionship alone was the pleasure I counted on this time, having so recently been satisfied in more exciting loves.

"My dear friend," she exclaimed, pressing both my hands in her own, "our feelings are perfectly reciprocal. A full course of love once a week is sufficient for me, and I am a little suspicious that my last one will satisfy me for a twelvemonth. Shall we retire?"

"With all my heart," I eagerly replied; and away we tripped to her private apartment.

We talked awhile about the old world folks, but the conversation very soon changed to that all-absorbing theme, which I need hardly to say was *love*. "Do you know," said she, "that now the passions are completely enfranchised, lovers give way to a very strong natural propensity, most blissful to indulge, which used to be but rarely hinted at either in verse or prose?"

"If it's a fair question," said I, "did my young friend, the poet, indulge in this dainty blissfulness?"

"You may be quite sure he did," she replied; "A man like him never spent a night with a woman like me without that enjoyment; the thing would be impossible; unless, as in the present case, it is but sociability and friendship that is desired."

"Well, well," said I, "" I did'nt think the fellow would go that length the first time. He is bolder and even more pasionate than I thought he was."

"His passion did a great deal," said she, "but his boldness seconded his passion so feebly, that he would not have accomplished his object but for a little timely assistance from myself. Never in my life before was I so highly amused. Again and again was he brought up *almost* to the right point, where his virgin coyness held him in check, till I was, as he thought, fast asleep. Then, * *
If his passion had not completely subjugated his reason, he could not have supposed any woman capable of remaining asleep, whilst being so strongly loved as I was. I indulged him till his extasies were as high as I dared to let them go for fear he would swoon, or otherwise injure himself, and then changed my position so that he had to desist; taking care to do so, without letting him suspect that I knew what he had been about.

In the morning, the conflict between his *mauvaise-*

honte and the powerful inclination recommenced. I watched my opportunity, and, just at the right time, I volunteered the little sweet force necessary to overcome the resistance he was so reluctantly exerting, help him to what women are as delighted to give as men are to receive, and make that gift as rich as it possibly could be."

"And you did'nt let on—did'nt even hint that you knew what he thought you did not know. Did you?"

"Perhaps I did, for I felt very roguish about it, I must confess. And when he was kissing me good morning, I said—my friend, when you and your 'partner for life' come to enjoy the 'honey moon,' do'nt reverse the order of that enjoyment."

"And how about these would be 'partners for life'—these 'constants'—does constancy now, in reality, ever stick to its profession?"

"Yes, the same as it always did. Constancy means uncommon constancy *to love itself*, and *therefore*, uncommon inconstancy to any one object of it. When people used to bind themselves to each other for life, it was generally the case that they who did so in the coldest and most conventional manner, stuck to each other the longest. By far the greatest number of divorces and separations took place among those cooing doves who had vowed eternal constancy with most ardour while they were tying on their chords."

"Do you know, said she, "that I am writing a series of love tales? I am going to give my experiences with some fifty or sixty different gallants, suopressing the names, of course, and I assure you that my adventure with the young poet will not be omitted."

"I long to read your book," said I, "for if it is well written, as I doubt not it will be, it will possess all the piquancy of a book of gallantry, without being associated with the meanness, rascality, nastiness, and loathsome disease that were necessarily associated with such books in the Dismal Ages. Then, a gallant tale always included brothers disgraced, husbands wronged and exposed to ridicule, and women or girls taken advantage of.

Charles The Second was called the "Merry Monarch;" and what did he do that made him so merry? Why, he spent his time in seducing barmaids and servant girls; often lavishing a diamond ring or a gold watch (at the nation's expense) on some wench that had long been the enjoyment of unwashed clowns. His Majesty was lucky if he did'nt get lousy or catch the itch: and it is quite clear that both he and his noble associates, and all others like them, often caught something a great deal worse than both.

"Kings and emperors very often freely mingled the royal semen with that of ostlers or boot blacks. As to their mistresses on whom they conferred titles of nobility, they were generally the wives of sated husbands; their stale favors were bought for a price, like any other commodity; and that was all the reciprocalness there was in the case. Now, all being perfectly healthy, and perfectly clean, there is nothing to be either feared or disgusted at in the matter of *free* gallantry; and, as women are situated beyond the possibility of being wronged, I should think your book would be the very acme of delightful reading; your stories will be incomparably more piquant than the spiciest of those wrttten by Brantome, Boccaccio, or even Margaret of Navarre."

"Will you please tell me some of those tales?" said she, "it may give me some useful hints in the arrangement of mine."

"A good idea," said I. "Well, let me see, which one shall I tell first? There's the '*Stratagem by which a Woman enabled her Gallant to escape, when her Husband, who was blind of an eye, thought to surprise them together.*' Then there's the '*Trick put by a Mercer of Paris on an Old Woman, to conceal his Intrigue with her daughter.*' The next I remember, is this: —'*A Gentleman finds his cruel Fair One in the arms of her Groom, and is cured at once of his Love.*' But I must begin somewhere, and will therefore tell you the story of the man who, in spite of the best safeguards that 'law' and 'morality' afforded, *accidentally made his own wife an adultress, and himself the most ridiculous of cuckolds.*

"There was in the country of Allez, a person named Bornet, who had married a virtuous wife, and held her honour and reputation dear, * *
* * * *

though he desired that his wife should be faithful to him, he did not choose to be equally bound to her; in fact, he made love to his servant, though all the good he could get by the change was the pleasure attending a diversity of viands. He had a neighbour, much of his own sort, named Sandras, a tailor by trade, with whom he was on terms of such close friendship, that everything was common between them except the wife. Accordingly Bornet declared the design he had formed upon the servant-girl to his friend, who not only approved of it, but did what he could for its success, in hopes of having a finger in the pie. But the servant would not hear of such a thing, and finding herself persecuted on all sides, she complained to her mistress, and begged to be allowed to go home to her relations, as she could no longer endure her master's importunity. The mistress, who was very fond of her husband, and who even before this had been jealous of him, was very glad to have this opportunity of reproaching him, and showing that it was not without reason she had suspected him. With this view she induced the servant to finesse with her master, give him hopes by degrees, and finally promise to let him come to bed to her in her mistress's wardrobe. 'The rest you may leave to me,' she said. 'I will take care that you shall not be troubled at all, provided you let me know the night he is to come to you, and that you do not breathe a syllable of the matter to any one living.'

"The girl faithfully obeyed her mistress's instructions, and her master was so delighted that he hastened at once to impart this good news to his friend, who begged that, since he had been concerned in the bargain, he should also partake of the pleasure. This being agreed to, and the hour being come, the master went to bed, as he supposed, with the servant; but the mistress had taken her place, and received him, not as a wife, but as a bashful and frightened maid; and she played her part so well, that he never suspected anything. I cannot tell you which of the two felt the greater satisfaction, he in the belief that he was cheating his wife, or she in the belief that she was cheating her husband.

"After he had remained with her not so long as he wished, but as long as he could, for he showed symptoms of an old married man, he went out of doors to his friend, who was younger and more vigorous, and told him what a fine treat he had just had. 'You know what you promised me,' said the friend. 'Well, be quick, then,' said the master, 'for fear she gets up, or my wife wants her.' The friend lost no time, but took the unoccupied place beside the supposed servant, who, thinking he was her husband, let him do whatever he liked without a word said on either side. He made a much longer business of it than the husband, greatly to the surprise of the wife, who was not accustomed to be so well regaled. However, she took it all patiently, comforting herself with the thought of what she would say to him in the morning, and how she would make game of him. The friend got out of bed towards daybreak, but not without taking the stirrup cup. During this ceremony he drew from her finger the ring with which her husband had wedded her, a thing which the women of that country preserve with great superstition, thinking highly of a woman who keeps it till death; on the other hand, one who has had the mischance to lose it is looked upon as having given her faith to another than her husband.

"When the friend had rejoined the husband, the latter asked him what he thought of his bedfellow

'Never was a better,' replied the friend; 'and if I had not been afraid of being surprised by daylight, I should not have come away from her so soon.' That said, they went to bed and slept as quietly as they could. In the morning, when they were dressing, the husband perceived on his friend's finger the ring, which looked very like that he had given his wife when he married her. He asked who had given him that ring, and was astounded to hear that he had taken it from the servant's finger. 'Oh Lord! have I made a cuckold of myself, without my wife's knowing it?' cried the husband, knocking his head against the wall. The friend suggested for his consolation that possibly his wife might have given the ring overnight to the servant to keep.

"Home goes the husband, and finds his wife looking handsomer and gayer than usual, delighted as she was to have hindered her servant from committing a sin, and to have convicted her husband without any more inconvenience to herself than to have passed a night without sleeping. The husband, seeing her in such good spirits, said to himself, 'She would not look so merry if she knew what has happened.' Falling into chat with her upon indifferent matters, he took her hand, and saw that the ring she always wore was not upon her finger. Aghast, and with a trembling voice, he asked her what she had done with it. This gave her the opportunity she was on the watch for to let loose upon him, and she seized it with avidity.

"'O, you most abominable of men!' she said, "from whom do you suppose you took it? You thought you had it from the servant. You thought it was for her you did more than you ever did for me. The first time you came to bed to her, I thought you made as much of her as it was possible to do; but after you left the room and came again the second time, it seemed as though you were the very devil of incontinence. What infatuation has possessed you to praise me so much, you wretch? You have had me long enough, and never cared about me. Is it the beauty and plumpness of your servant that made the pleasure seem so sweet to you? No, base man, it is the fire of your own disorderly lust that makes you so blindly in love with the servant, that in the furious fit you were in, I believe you would have taken a she-goat with a nightcap for a fine girl. It is high time, husband, that you should mend your ways, and content yourself with me who am your wife, and, as you know, an honest woman, as much as you did when you mistook me for a vicious woman. My only object in the matter has been to withdraw you from vice, so that in our old days we may live in amity and repose of conscience; for if you choose to continue the life you have led hitherto, I would rather we should separate than that I should see you daily treading the path that leads to hell, and at the same time using up your body and your substance. But if you resolve to behave better, and to fear God and keep his commandments. I am willing to forget the past, as I trust God will forgive the ingratitude I am guilty of in not loving him as much as I ought.'

"If ever a man was confounded and horrified, it was the poor husband. It was bad enough to think that he had forsaken his wife, who was fair, chaste and virtuous, and overflowing with affection for him, for a woman who did not love him; but it was infinitely worse when he represented to himself that he had been so unlucky as to make her quit the path of virtue, in spite of herself, and without knowing it, to share with another the pleasures which should have been his alone, and to have forged for himself the horns of perpetual mockery. Seeing, however, that his wife was already angry enough about his intended intrigue with the servant, he did not dare to tell her of the villainous trick he had played upon herself. He implored her pardon, promised to make amends for the past by the strictest propriety of conduct in future, and gave her back her ring, which he had taken from his friend, whom he begged not to say a word of what had happened. But as everything whispered in the ear is by-and-by proclaimed from the house-top, the adventure became public at last, and people called him a cuckold, without any regard for his wife's feelings."

"Pray," said the lady, " to whom are we indebted for this precious bit of literary spice ?"

" The origin of the story is rather obscure," I replied. " We can trace it to the fabliau of *Le Meunier d'Alens*; it occurs in the facetiæ of Poggio, in Sachetti, in the *Cent Nouvelles Nouvelles*, and in the *Heptameron of Margaret, Queen of Navarre*."

Several hundred years thereafter, a somewhat similar affair occurred on board a steamboat. " A gentleman," says the relator, " had made arrangements for the chambermaid to come to his stateroom; after the other passengers had turned in, and the lights were extinguished, he left his door ajar, for her to enter. The next room to his was occupied by a very respectable married couple. The lady being taken short in the night slipped out without waking her husband, also leaving the door-ajar. On returning, she took the wrong door, and closed it after her; the maid entered the other door, and whilst she was wondering at the coldness of her reception, the wife was being too well entertained to remain long ignorant of her part of the mistake. Such a time you never saw. The scene was so pitiful that I came off without waiting to see how it terminated."

"What seems most incredible in Dismal Age literature is the fact that people *generally* made sport of marriage, and, in their most popular novels and plays, ridiculed it to the lowest degree, yet held it to be ordained of "God," or else the most sacred and important of civil institutions. Nothing in the great religious, moral, political, and social hodge-podge, seems to me to be quite so absurd as this," remarked the lady.

"Begging your pardon, my love," said I, " I believe I can point out something in that wilderness of inconsistency a little more absurd, and a good deal more abominable. All the gods, goddesses, demi-gods, and demi-goddesses, held up for worship in 'civilized' ages, *were begotten out of wedlock*. Moreover, the Jewish God, afterwards adopted by the Christians, had, according to the 'Holy Writ,' three special favourites :— Abraham, David, and Solomon. The first twice introduced his wife to certain lecherous old kings for his sister, each time receiving large rewards for her prostitution. The second, whom we are told, on divine authority, was a man after God's own heart, ordered a husband to be sent where he would certainly be killed, in order to get possession of that husband's wife. The third, all the Christian boys and girls were taught to consider the wisest man that had been or could be; they were taught that Jehovah [the man after his own heart had the impudence to nickname him *Jah*] himself said so. Yet that man had 700 wives and 300 concubines. A 699th part of that man's offence would have consigned him to the penitentiary, according to a law which these same boys and girls were taught to respect, and bound to observe when they became men and women!"

"Can it be possible that our ancestors were thus ignorant, inconsistent, and debased?" observed the lady; "but I know they were. I am well enough versed in antiquity to be assured of that. And they didn't seem to entertain the idea of *positive* pleasure; and, in fact, such a thing was scarcely known to them. For instance, their pleasantest method of voyaging or journeying was scarcely comfortable; it gave so little *positive* enjoyment that when they had fair weather during a trip across the sea, they grumbled all the way, and never thanked 'God' for it; but if they had a storm that came near sending them to 'Davy Jones's locker,' how joyously and profusely they sent forth their praises to the brave captain, the faithful crew, and their 'Heavenly Father.' It was the storm that these poor wretches really thanked; it broke monotony; than which nothing is less endurable; no wonder they ran into the idea that pain and evil were necessary. Also, in their amours, as they could have no variety without *stealing* it, they concluded that it was *theft* and not *change* that gave those amours their piquancy. *The* wise man has laid it down as an axiom that 'stolen waters—meaning ladies' favors unlawfully obtained—are sweet,' and that settled the question with them. But I think I could instantly have put an end to their philosophy. I was lately reading in *Count Grammont's Amours of Charles the Second and his Court*, how the lords and ladies of that gayest Court of the Dismal Age, descended to the position of quack mediciners, fortune-tellers, and orange girls, in order to gratify their lustfulness, and to dispel their *ennui*. How one of those ladies 'shewed her leg above the knee,' whereat the numerous lords and gentlemen present were ready to prostrate themselves in order to adore its beauty! How the duke was sitting next to her [Lady Chesterfield] * * * no one could see his arm below the elbow. * * The duke was so much disturbed that he almost undressed my lady in pulling away his hands;'—all which was delightfully piquant because it involved slyness and theft, as was supposed. But if that duke was alive now, and could get his hand under *my* crinoline, without theft, intrigue, or meanness of any sort, don't you think he would be better pleased than he was when fumbling like a pick-pocket beneath the thick draggled skirts and old fashion-scented chemise of Lady Chesterfield? And if King Charles' courtiers could see *my* leg, don't you think they would be convinced that there was such a thing as *positive pleasure?*" she added, giving me a glance from her sparkling eyes that sent thrills of inexpressible delight through my whole frame.

"I believe," said I, "that if King Solomon himself were in my place, *just at this moment*, his Majesty would swoon with delight, confess his famous proverb about ' *stolen waters*' to be the offspring of a low, contemptible, and wretchedly depraved taste, and own that his other saw about all being 'vanity and vexation,' was the braying of an ass. I don't believe there ever was a Jew, Turk, Pagan, or Christian, who would not eagerly part for ever with wives, concubines, mistresses, sly pieces, and all, for a single night with yourself, or any other woman who now exists."

"And I had rather be killed this moment," said the beauty, shuddering, "than endure a night with any Pagan, Mahommedan, Israelite, or Christian, that ever lived, judging from the best portraits and most reliable histories of them."

Next day the Grand Artist determined to restore the six remaining old fogies to their consciousness; and in such a way as to afford us a great treat.

The people were early notified of his plan, and the balloons were soon in readiness.

The six sleepers were placed in His Highness's balloon car; the ladies and gentlemen were quickly seated in this and the other balloon cars, and up we went.

At just the height that afforded the most favorable view, the sleepers were placed so as to face that view, and the galvanic battery was applied to them. Its first shock fully restored them to their senses.

"Where are we?" they all faintly ejaculated, staring around in utter astonishment.

"Why, in Heaven to be sure," I answered.

"But I don't see God," said the parson.

"Yes you do," replied the Grand Artist. "Put the other o into that 'Word'* as you should do, and look again."

"Poh! I do'nt believe in God," interrupted the bewildered skeptic, trembling all over, and scarcely able to articulate, for fear there was one after all.

"No", said I, "You skeptics only believe in the Devil with the D omitted, and the word 'necessary' prefixed. Skeptics and moralists, by trying to reconcile mankind with 'necessary evil' have been a greater bar to the perfection you now behold, than the blindest fanatics that ever mumbled a creed."

By this time the old fogies had discovered that they were in the flesh, and their courage revived accordingly.

"But what we mainly insisted on was 'duty;'— we exhorted people to do as they would be done by, and tried to compel the refractory to observe our golden rule; you can't object to duty or 'the golden rule,' anyhow," stammered the moralist.

"Duty and the Golden Rule are as different as any two things can be," said I. "You violated the golden rule to the utmost possible extent; we thoroughly practice it. As to 'duty,' it is a word utterly without sense; it is pure *cant*; it may now be seen in a very ancient dictionary in our great Museum. But it is out of use, and forever will be.

---

* "And the Word *was* God." *St. John.*

Duty, or, as it was sometimes called, 'self-denial,' was double and twisted self-deception. No man or woman ever acted on the duty principle; they never *absolutely* denied themselves *any* gratification whatever. All they did in the case was to choose according to their temperaments or other circumstances; between this and that gratification, or what they supposed was, or would be such. All the 'moral philosophy' that has ever been preached, written, or sung, practically sums up in the soliloquy of the fox who couldn't get the grapes. All the praise bestowed on 'self-denial' was justly due to ignorance of the means of *self-gratification*. Here, in 'Heaven,' we don't follow virtue even for virtue's sake; simply because ignorance with respect to physical law is so thoroughly abolished that there is no necessity for doing so. *Nature, through art, has at length provided the means of following our own inclinations to the benefit instead of injury of each other.* We go by the law that we feel is from our maker, but which 'duty' so long and so mischievously opposed.

No sooner was the subject of "duty" introduced, than all the "old fogies" began chewing their tobacco as if to make up for centuries of lost time.

We had especially provided spittoons for their accommodation, but they paid little regard to them, spitting all over the velvet carpet till the ladies began to heave at the stomach.

"Sorry tobacco is so offensive to the company," said the parson; and the whole dirty gang similarly apologised, at the same time squirting their spittle overboard in such a shower that we had to telegraph down for the people to stand from under.

It was now the lawyers' turn.

"What!" he exclaimed, "surely you don't mean what you say about duty! Why, duty is the fundamental principle of *civil law*, that only preservative from utter licentiousness and anarchy. You haven't abolished all statutes, I hope; and what is the use of them, except to compel people to perform their duties? What would the world come to if evil-minded people were not thus compelled? What *would* society be if everybody was let loose from all constraint?"

"Why, just what you see it is," answered I. "Yes, just what you see it is," repeated a nymph of ravishing beauty, ensconcing herself most bewitchingly in the arms of her lover. "There are no evil-minded people in the world now, and never were, for that matter," she continued; "The worst desires ever entertained were, at bottom, for happiness. All the evil in the case arose from *ignorance as to method;* but that is all got along with now, you see."

By this time the gammon laboratory of the politician was in working order.

"Is this a monarchy or a democracy?" he asked, eagerly scanning the rich field for official theft and swindling, which the prospect all around seemed to present, and hurriedly demanding to see *The Constitution*.

"For mercy's sake," said I, "don't mention *The Constitution*. It was the most deceptive and mischievous swindle ever palmed off on human folly.

According to the Constitution, government and people were required to act, not according to current circumstances, but according to *past* conditions. The Constitution was the rule (strange that Hoyle should have omitted it), according to which demagogues or political gamblers played their most atrocious game of Caucus and Ballot-Box; national spoliation being the stakes. Even in *common* gambling when bets ran high, the losers, rather than disgorge, often used dirks and revolvers, instead of cards and dice. So, in the game of Caucus and Ballot Box. When one set of demagogues won the pilfering of a nation's treasury for a long time hand-running, so soon as luck changed sides, Armstrong guns and iron-clad steam rams wound up the play. Monarchy used to be bad enough, but Caucus and Ballot Box—*alias* Constitutionalism—was the shortest cut to ruin that a nation ever took. It was a perfect liberty-mockery. It made the people the tools for placing in power this or that nominee for their own spoliation, for from one to four years, and then gave a new and ungorged horde of political vampires their turn; for quick 'rotation in office' was one of The Constitution's fundamental principles. No people ever endured The Constitution and its Caucus and Ballot Box long at a time."

" But the long and short of it is, that there never was a ' Constitution.' Your so-called ' Constitution,' and its correlate, named ' elective franchise,' were as pure delusions as were your ' immaterial,' ' God,' and your ' supernatural' ' religion.' One party said the ' Constitution' was *this ;* the other party said it was *that,* and the ' elective franchise' *prac-*

tically dwindled down into scatteringly throwing your ballots into the box as vainly as if you had thrown them into the fire, or drawing in the traces of the *nominators*, who had no other aim than theft, and whose nominees, were they ever so well inclined, could do nothing but ' pave hell' with good intentions.' It was under the most honest of the ' elected,' that the people suffered most ; the elect, who were stupid enough to be sincere in such a scheme, were sure to be the most foolish, and foolishness was the cause of all the suffering that ever was or ever could be. When either party became dissatisfied with their luck at the constitutional game of caucus and ballot-box, and were strong enough to refuse to abide by their losses at that game, what availed the ' Constitution?' Did it not *then*, and in *that* case, *always* prove to be a myth ? Did it not invariably, and times without number, serve those who, *in time of need*, leaned on it for support, as falsely as they would have been served if they had leaned on their own shadows ?"

" No," said the politician; "I maintain that the Constitution long guarded the United States from such oppression and wrong as Spain, Russia, and other non-constitutional countries were subjected to."

" And I maintain," said I, " that it was *superior natural position*, and *superior advantages as to physical science and art*, that gave the United States all the good they possessed more than other countries. As to majorityism, could it have been honestly carried into practice, the result would have proved that the powers below in *this* world, like the powers below, in the ' world to come,' are by far the most dreadful."

"If mankind had only been governed by reason, all would have been well," chimed in the skeptic.

"Alas, for poor, impotent reason," said I. "Reason does very little, except to choose between these and those circumstances, and try to acquiesce under them. It is instinct—desire—*passion*, that pushes ahead, whilst science and art clear the way."

"Perhaps our new friends would like to be taken back to their wives and children, or have their families sent for," said one of the ladies, pityingly.

At this suggestion, the poor old fogies most heartily wished their dear wives and children had a separate maintenance provided, and that the moral law was consigned to the "Devil." In fact, there was not one of them who could be safely trusted with his neighbor's wife or daughter, provided she was willing, or could, by the most unfair means be made so, and there was a bed, sofa, or sly hay-cock handy. How lustfully they gazed on the ravishing beauties before them—how recklessly they committed the kind of adultery most severely censured in Scripture* I leave the reader to imagine.

"Don't put yourselves to any inconvenience on account of our families," said the unbeliever.

"Oh no; there's no hurry in the case," quickly added the others.

"Who is the Emperor, King, President or Overseer of this magnificent country?" asked the political economist.

"I can answer for him," replied the Grand Artist.

---

* See Mathew, V. 28.

"I should think you had more business on hand than half the world could attend to. How do you manage to preserve any kind of order amidst such outrageous and anarchical principles?—principles and practices which to put down used to require an extensive police, and magistracy, backed by immense armies?"

"And what success did your police, magistracy and armies achieve?" asked the Grand Artist. "Did not every sort of irregularity and atrociousness grow up under them, and, ever and anon, burst into carnivals unsurpassably horrible? If I had to see to all the details of government, there could not be the order and magnificence and universal well-being there is, by a dreadful odds. It's an easier matter to conduct the affairs of this country, vast and well-regulated as it is, than it used to be to manage a school district. The social machine once right, can by no possibility get wrong. Right is now *immutably established on selfishness*, the greatest bugbear of the Dismal Ages, and on *positive knowledge*, which our silly forefathers so feared would lead to atheism.

"Rulers are now wide awake to the great truth that the best—the *only* way to secure their own welfare is to secure the welfare of all; they have got into the way of doing that all-important thing, and they can no more get out of it than the planets can break from their orbits.

"It used to be thought impossible—"utopian"— that the present magnificent system of universal good could be *realized;* only a few could form a clear preconception of it, and that preconception was sneered at as *mere theory*—as if there *could be theory to what was impossible in practice!* But were it not that history tells us *how* the old system of universal wrong and evil was instituted and kept up, *not one* of us could understand it, or believe it possible.—*How could we imagine* that mankind ever composed armies—in some instances *"en masse"*—to rob, maim and slaughter, instead of enriching, preserving, and gratifying each other ? that they would 'enlist' and combine to freeze, starve, break the limbs, knock out the brains, and rip up the bowels of their fellow-men, instead of enlisting and combining to have all they want as long as they please.

"A few hundred 'Hell'-hounds could *combine,* and *thus* create a center of *infernal* motion that all the world had to follow, *nolens-volens.* We cannot imagine a *stranger* —a more *impossible* thing, than that mankind's leaders should have been so long in discovering the present social system—discovering that it would be incomparably easier, and infinitely more *profitable for themselves,* to form a center of "Heavenly" motion—an immutable system of freedom-perfecting statics and dynamics, than to keep up their murderous hodge-podge of social wrong, misery, and revolution.

With the people, this reciprocalness of interests is a creed; and reliance on their leaders, whom *they know cannot betray them*, is a habit that can no more be overcome than gravitation can be abolished.

In astro-physics, all revolves around a mathematical point—a mere nothing. In social physics, the head or center of all, though absolutely indispensable, and absolutely necessary—though *seeming* to wield an almighty influence, has not much to do himself; infinitely less than, at first sight, would be supposed. The great social machine runs spontancously, as I have just remarked. It always did, for that matter; but now, *its spontaneity has accomplished its end—the production of harmony, and perfect, universal and immutable freedom.*"

"Still," said the politician, "I can't but think that it would be safer to have a *constitutional* check on the ambition or caprice of rulers; see what horrors they perpetrated in Spain, France, Turkey, and wher ever there was no Constitution!"

Here the whole assembly, except the old fogies, simultaneously burst into the most singular laugh that I ever heard; a laugh that instantly ended in silent gloom.

"Did the rulers of Spain, Italy, Dahomey, or any other country, ever perpetrate anything so cruel, unjust, tyrannical, and utterly abhorrent as secession?" replied the Grand Artist. "The Constitution was a parasitical fungus that sprouted out of mysticism and moralism, after the legitimate tree, absolutism, was cut down. The most opposite factions in demagoguery clung to the "Constitution" as the most opposite sects of "Protestantism did to the 'Bible;' and they all claimed to be the bulwarks of 'Civilization'; whereas, they were the clogs, the very Nemesis to all that was good in that distracted compound."

"But did not civilization flourish most gloriously in Protestant America, and under demagoguery: as you call it?" retorted the politician.

"If all the good that material art was the means of, had been deducted from civilization," said the

Grand Artist, "what would have remained? It was material art that did all the good then, and it is material art that has eliminated everything but good."

"But are the people free here? Do they enjoy freedom of speech, freedom of the press, free trade, and, above all, mental freedom?" inquired the politician.

"We don't know anything about 'mental freedom' here; with us everything is physical, or functional of physicalness. The people are free to do everything except to destroy their own freedom. They were free to do little else than that in the Dismal Ages. Now, *without the exercise of any arbitrary power*, they are not free to beget children under such circumstances as to populate the world with beings either 'totally depraved,' or in the slightest degree faulty. They are not free to poison their children, and, through them, unborn generations, with unwholesome food; nor to spoil their blood, and rot their lungs, and soften their brains, with bad air. They are not free, *as they used to be*, to build houses and public conveyances apparently for that especial purpose. They are not free to carry raw material four thousand miles, to be manufactured and brought back at their expense, whilst they go barefooted, and work like mules to pay that expense. The people have every liberty except that which, according to the old story, the 'apostate angels' fought so desperately for—the liberty to go to 'hell,' drag all their connections thither, and entail damnation on posterity. It is now just as impossible for people to do wrong as it is for matter to disobey the law of gravitation."

"And what power decides under what conditions the people shall be begotten, what they shall eat and drink, what they shall wear—beg pardon, I see they wear next to nothing—what houses they shall live in, what conveyances they shall go in, and everything else?" asked the infidel.

"The scientists and artists, whose business it is to discover the best solutions of these questions, and see those discoveries put in practice," was His Highness's reply.

"Are you at liberty to kiss me, my dear?" asked the parson, of a little girl not yet in her teens.

"No, sir," she mildly answered with a pleasant smile.

"And why not?" continued the parson.

"Because I don't want to," was the naive and perfectly unsophisticated reply.

"Here," said the parson, "I've got you. This little girl has hurt my feelings; don't you call that wrong? Can you pretend that all is *now* good and right?"

"If it wasn't for hurting your feelings again," answered the Grand Artist, "I would remind you that you are not a part of the perfection in question, but an accident that can go no further, and can't last long."

"But if she had kissed me, she would not have hurt my feelings," rejoined the parson.

"But she would have hurt her own feelings, and that would have been quite as bad, would it not?" I replied. "The apostles of 'self-denial' did not take into their calculation the fact that self-injury is just as injurious as any other injury. They approved of self-injury to any extent short of instant self-killing, and that they considered worse than ten thousand other murders, and absolutely unpardonable."

"Well, how do you manage so as to always avoid the alternative of injuring either self or somebody else?" asked the moralist.

"By a rule of universal application. By a religio-political system, based on material art, that embraces the whole world; no narrower system could do that," replied the Grand Artist.

"The whole world!" exclaimed all the old fogies, in chorus.

"Yes, the whole world," answered the Grand Artist. "My friend—pointing to me—told the literal truth when he said you were in Heaven. You are in Heaven on Earth. You have seen 'God'; at least, you have seen as much of Omnipotent Goodness as can be taken in at one view. You have also seen the 'glorified saints,' and now we will introduce you to the 'holy angels,' hoping you will find their 'ministrations' pleasant and 'edifying.'"

"Yes, I think our friends had better be introduced into one of our infant schools," suggested several of the company almost simultaneously, and the balloon was thereupon lowered, so that we alighted in the midst of one of those schools, situated in a flowery mead, tastefully shaded with trees, where the children, real flesh and blood "angels" recited the following lesson of the "Primary Catechism:"—

Question. Wherein consists the value of all existence?

Answer. In happiness.

Q. To what should all human endeavour, therefore, aim ?

A. To the acquisition, perfection, and sufficient prolongation of happiness.

Q. How do you know that happiness is *rightly* the sole object for which you should strive ?

A. I *feel* it to be so. *I cannot* desire anything else. Besides, there is nothing else worth living for.

Q. Is it right for you to strive to promote *only your own* happiness ?

A. It is.

Q. How do you know it to be right ?

A. From the fact that it is impossible for me voluntarily to strive for anything else.

Q. What guaranty have mankind always had, that perfect and sufficiently *lasting* happiness as to the *individual*, and perfect and *eternal* happiness as to the *species*, were attainable ?

A. Almighty Nature's ; whose highest consciousness and intelligence man is. The seed, the hope, the glimmering foreknowledge, of the great harvest of happiness which we are now reaping, nature planted in man, when, through development, she first rough-created him; and so deep, that it never could be uprooted, but must necessarily come, as it now has, to *full* maturity, to complete verification, where, in virtue of nature's *law of laws*, it *must* remain, as *inexhaustible* as the *race* of man is *eternal ;* as perpetual as is the equilibrium of the celestial spheroids.

Q. During the age of mystery, "morality," and

wretchedness, when man was in his primitive imperfection, in his physical and therefore intellectual heterogeneity—what name did his bewildered imagination give to the object of his *individual* existence?

A. *Eternal* happiness.

Q. Wherein consisted his mistake?

A. In not comprehending the Social Organism, or *collective* man—The *Eternal Being* to whom alone *eternal happiness can be happiness;* and in not knowing that temporal happiness could be made to last *long enough* to be *quite sufficient* for the *temporal* beings, which, through nature's law of individual change, successively constitute *eternal* Humanity.

Q. What *were* mystery, morality, and their correlative politics?

A. *The parasitical social fungus that almost overwhelmed science and art in the Dismal Ages, and usurped the name of " civilization."*

Q. How do you know that our present harvest of perfect happiness is inexhaustible, and that *our race* is fixed in eternal happiness?

A. The laws of intellectuality follow those of physicalness, on which they depend; and the Social Organism is now as harmoniously, and therefore as permanently, adjusted to all in its connection as is the solar system. Man's—nature's—spontaneous yearning for satisfaction has, aided by all in the connection, produced in the world of man, that *necessarily eternal* order which answers to the *equilibrium* which gravitation has, thus aided, produced in the planetary world. The *eternal* hap piness of collective man, and the perfect and sufficiently lasting happiness of *individual* man are, therefore, as assured as is the order of the celestial spheroids.

Q. In what relation do you stand toward all mankind ?

A. All mankind, from the first inseparably, though for a long time heterogeneously connected, are now happily, a harmoniously organized whole; of which I am a part, in as *strict* sympathy with all the other parts, as the most minute tissues of my body are in sympathy with all the rest of it.

Q. It seems then, that you cannot do an act which will promote your own happiness, without *simultaneously* doing one which *must* promote the good of all mankind; nor can you do an act fraught with evil to others, which will not *surely* redound to your own hurt, and this is the case with every human being. Do you comprehend all this ?

A. As easily as I understand that my whole body shares the sensation of dissatisfaction caused by the prick of a needle on the end of my little finger, or that of satisfaction, caused by the contact of my palate with food ; or that of delight, caused by my eyes beholding, my ears hearing, and my brains understanding, the pleasure which all around me experience.

Q. But though you are as *really*, you are not as *closely* connected with the rest of mankind, as the parts of your body are with yourself. How does the body politic immediately bring its all-sufficient power to bear in preventing wrong action ?

A. By means of that body's nerves and brain—

its Scientific Discoverers and Directors. By means of these, I acquire the aid of the whole force of the body politic and of all else in the connection, and am thus enabled to shape my actions in accordance with the Social Organism's welfare, and simultaneously with the welfare of every part of it, necessarily including myself. My functions, like those of the *mass* of mankind, are special; those of a few, but *naturally* sufficient number, are general.

Q. Are you and your compeers who compose the mass of mankind, then, but mere blind followers of your superiors?

A. Blind? no, indeed. Our *understandings*, and particularly our *feelings*, are constantly wide awake to the *results* which acting in accordance with the directions of our social functionaries produces. For the rest, we *have no superiors* in any *arbitrary* sense of the word.

Q. But what guaranty have you that these functionaries will not misguide you, or shape your action for their own special benefit?

A. They can no more be benefited by injuring us, than my individual nerves and brain can be benefited by damaging my muscles; *and they know it.* They know that our wretchedness would necessitate their misery; that their misery would be deeper and keener than our's; that the only other difference between their woes and our's would be that their's would be gilded and our's but varnished. We, the masses, have the same guaranty that our Scientific Discoverers and Directors will not wrong us, that my hand has, that my nerves and brain will not misdirect it into the fire.

As the lesson ended, fairy-like music, both vocal and instrumental, charmed the old fogies for the first time. In fact, the singing of these angelic children affected even myself more pleasantly than any melody I had yet heard.

"You see," said the Grand Artist, to the old fogies, "that the *general* principles of our system are so plain that children comprehend them. But did *any* one ever understand *anything whatever* respecting your so-called system, except that it made people as miserable as the physical science and art therein *stealthily* contained would allow them to be ? Why, there was more written to try to explain the 'religion' and 'law' that you expected every man and woman to act up to, than any one of them could have read in a thousand years. You further see that now, all do right without compulsion ; you expected they would, in 'Heaven,' did you not ?"

"Of course ; for we didn't expect people would carry their evil desires to Heaven," answered the parson.

"Nor have they done so," said His Highness ; "for the very good reason that they never had any evil desires. Evil desires are an absolute impossibility. 'The ' Devil' himself could not desire anymore than happiness. Jeff. Davis and his traitorous gang desired nothing more nor less than happiness ; but they ignorantly took the wrong, *the worst possible*, way, like all other 'smart' fools, to get it. The whole Social Organism now takes care of its parts, and does it perfectly. Nothing short of the *combined power of this great whole can do this*. The stupidest asses that ever lived showed their blindest stupidity in exhorting people *individually* to reform themselves; they might better have insisted that every individual man and woman should build their own railroad and steamship. The strangest thing to us now is, how people could have been so long in discovering that the only evil was want; the only remedy *the satisfaction of that want*, WITH JUST THE EXERTION REQUISITE TO GIVE DUE PLEASURABLENESS TO SATISFACTION."

"Apropos of this," said I, "permit me to relate how our pious ancestors laid their stupid blunders to the charge of their 'God.' For instance:—City railroad corporations piled on extortion and imposition till the people, unable to endure any more, smashed the cars and tore up the rails, killing and wounding scores of men and a number of women and children. 'God has taught unscrupulous greed of gain a good lesson,' drawled the long-visaged, hypocritical scoundrels, who pocketed the Lobby's bribes to legislate these very roads, with all their inducements to wrong, into existence.

When Secession, with its unprecedented horrors, broke out, 'had not God, in his inscrutable wisdom, visited us with this great calamity, we should have fallen into a condition lower than the Chinese, *through too much material prosperity*,' said a notable mouthpiece of the very politicians, whose *inscrutable knavery and foolishness* were at the bottom of the whole thing.

'The Bull Run defeat was, in the workings of

'divine providence,' 'all for the best;' it necessitated the President's emancipation policy;' was a favourite tune which cant gave out for stupidity to to sing. And stupidity couldn't see that it was that most undivine of all providences, stupidity itself, which prevented emancipation from unnecessitating the Bull Run slaughter. And this canting, hypocritical, miserable optimism went on thus till the Good Time put an end to it.

"I hardly think the old maids of those days believed it all for the best; even the silliest of them didn't *feel* as though it was, I'll be bound," added one of the ladies.

This remark threw a shade of sadness over all the company except the old fogies; but these depraved wretches grinned; some of them laughed outright at this allusion to the most unfortunate victims of Dismal Age cruelty.

"Well, my sweet child," said the parson, addressing the little girl he had asked to kiss him; "here's a gold dollar for you, to buy candy with; are we friends now?"

"What in the world is it?" asked several young lads and lasses, huddling around the curiosity.

As I perceived that most of the older members of the society present were as ignorant as the children were as to this gold dollar, I told them that it was the money of the Dismal Ages. That had the out and out democrats had the exclusive management of the "currency," only half the people in the world would have been engaged in the production of property of *actual* value, whilst the other half were engaged in making these dollars, or their equivalents in silver and copper, to measure actual value with. To do these out and outers justice, however, it must be stated that; in their day, paper did not represent useful, ornamental, and amusing productions, but an army of shinplaster barons and their retainers, whose most useful business was to contrive how to carry on the cheat of shuffling the gold about, so that it should be at the point where paper demanded it, until *such a rush of paper was made at some such point that it would be less profitable to these barons and their retainers to have the gold there than to withdraw it altogether, and burst up, or* "*fail.*" The only other *certain* basis of paper money in the Dismal Ages was *whole territories richly manured by human blood, brains, bones, and sinews! through war ! !*

After a delicious dinner, produced as if by enchantment, in the sumptuous eating saloon of the palace, they visited many other palaces, the bureaus of departments, libraries, museums, gymnasiums, theatres, schools, and the Grand Temple, where the glorious Gospel of Science was preached (on this temple the truly Catholic inscription was, "*Ars Antium Hominorum Salvator est*); and last, and most interesting of all, the nurseries.

The lying-in apartments of these were very far superior to the accouchement chambers of queens and empresses in days of yore. The accommodations for *all* children were incomparably better than any royal progeny had ever been provided with. Parents had no individual responsibility on account of their off-spring. Mothers nursed their young as long as they pleased, and both fathers and mothers could gratify their taste for child-fondling whenever they felt so inclined, without being kept awake nights by squalling young ones, and without being saturated with a liquid, smelling very different from rose-water, and with semi liquids, most abominably resembling custard and blanc mange. Fondling one's own darlings, it hardly need be observed, was a pleasure which fathers were never quite perfectly assured of, but if that was any satisfaction, it could now be enjoyed more confidently than ever it could be in the Dismal Ages; as mothers, when free, invariably put the father's mark on the child. But this is scarcely worth mentioning, for, in reality, it is not of the slightest consequence.

"How incalculably expensive all this must be," observed the political economist.

"Expensive? why, it costs just nothing at all,' replied the Grand Artist. "The cost of a thing is the *pains* taken to produce it. The *perfection* you behold is, as you see, produced by *clear pleasure*. The 'Hell' system was, indeed, expensive. In 1862, and for some years thereafter, the demagogue-phase of infernalism (being in one of its periodical crises) cost the United States alone, more than it would to have established 'Heaven' on earth."

"But I should think the world would be overpopulated with such facilities for propagation as you have established," remarked the political economist.

"Did you never observe," answered I, "that, even in the Dismal Ages, those in the lowest scale of humanity, begat twice as many children as did those in the highest. Without going into minute particulars, I tell you now, as I always did, that Nature's—the Almighty's—means are adequate to produce the greatest ends, that she signifies through man, her highest organ of desire."

"How were the masses educated up to the point of adopting your form of government?" asked the politician.

"Ay, it must have taken a long course of schooling and free discussion, to enlighten them to that degree," continued the skeptic.

"Educating the 'masses' and indiscriminate free discussion, had precious little to do in the matter," said the Grand Artist. "The masses, even now, understand no more about religion and government *in the concrete*, than the cabin passengers in the Great Eastern knew how to build and navigate that magnificent steamer. The masses follow leaders, as inevitably as the planets revolve around the sun's centre. Long before these leaders had become fully convinced that by no possible trickery could they acquire any good at the expense of the body-politic, the scientists and artists were on hand with the rudiments of the great system you now see in universally successful operation."

"And how was supernaturalism got out of the people's heads?" asked the skeptic.

"They never had *it* in," replied the Grand Artist. "They blindly received as religion a sophistically-woven tissue of impossibleness, of course without proof, and they rejected all such nonsense for the Religion of Science, so soon as the clergy preached the latter instead of the former. I tell you that the people follow leaders, as naturally as sheep follow the bell-weather. Unbelievers, by arguing as they did, against supernaturalism, impliedly admitted that there was such a thing; they admitted that people believed it—thought of it—had *some* knowledge of it."

"Well," said the skeptic, impatiently, "pray tell us how the people's leaders found the right path."

"You shall know this all in good time," replied the Grand Artist.

But free-love was what the old fogies were most horrified at.

"It's very clear that you don't believe in future punishment, or you wouldn't give your passions the reins, as you do," said the parson.

"Of course we don't believe in future punishment," I replied; "I fully admit your premises, but can't see the justice of your conclusion. Did the fear of *eternal Hell-fire*, even when it was most firmly entertained, prevent the most *orthodox teachers* of that horrible doctrine from giving *their* passions the reins? If the company would like to hear it, I will tell a story apropos of this, that was written in the Dismal Ages by Boccacio. It forms part of *The Decameron*."

"Oh, for decency's sake, if you have any left, don't mention *The Decameron*," said the parson.

The parson's answer raised a suspicion in my mind.

"My Reverend friend," said I, "will you please to favor me with your autograph?"

The hypocrite wrote it on a scrap of paper which I presented. Instantly, I recognised the handwriting and the name. This very parson had, when I was in my former state, publishing books at No. 30 Ann Street, New York, wrote to me for *The Decameron*, and he charged me so strictly to send it "*carefully sealed from impertinent curiosity*," that I remembered the circumstance.

"Do tell us the story," said the gentlemen. "Oh, do, please tell us this story about the olden time," chimed in half a dozen ladies at once.

After whispering something in the parson's ear, which, the reader can easily guess, kept his reverence quiet, I began as follows :—

Ladies and Gentlemen—

I shall not tell the story *verbatim* ; the outlines will be quite sufficient for my present purpose.

In order to fully understand what I am going to relate, you must know that "once upon a time" people were so completely besotted by the fear of future punishment, that thousands retired to the deserts to wear out their lives in fasting, prayer, and love-mortification. Love-indulgence was considered so exceedingly dangerous to the "soul's" everlasting welfare, that many instances of "self-emasculation took place. "The Messiah" had given out that this was highly commendable ; he almost as good as said that it was a perfect assurance of a place in the "Kingdom of Heaven."

A young Mahommedan girl, all innocence and simplicity, who lived near the confines of Christendom, got her devotion, fear, and curiosity, so aroused by the reports she heard of the Christians, and how they served God in the wilderness, that she boldly determined to find out whether or not there was a better and surer way to salvation than the one she had been taught to believe in.

Early one morning young Alibech stole away from her parents, and at night asked and obtained admittance to the cell of a very pious hermit named Rusticus. She told him that, inspired by God, she had come to learn the Christian way to Heaven.

Before I proceed further, Ladies and Gentlemen, I must inform you that it was a prevalent maxim with the fathers of the Christian Church, that the merit of resisting love-gratification depended on the strength of the temptation thereto. To such an extent was this theory carried into practice, that, says Gibbon, " The virgins of the warm climate of Africa permitted priests and deacons to share their bed, and gloried amidst the flames in their unsullied purity." But notwithstanding their glorying, and in spite of " Hell's hot jurisdiction," the historian just named informs us that the flesh conquered the spirit so often that the temptation experiment had to be given up.

But to go on with the story :

No sooner did the devout Rusticus behold the fair Alibech, than he considered her the special providence of God, and he resolved to improve so favorable an opportunity for letting the Devil know how utterly he despised, and how little he feared him.

But while he was contriving how to manage in putting his experiment into operation, the Devil assaulted him so violently, that, instead of discipline and holy thoughts, he found himself ruminating on the youth and beauty of the fair pilgrim, and devising by what means he should satisfy the desires she raised in him.

He told Alibech that serving God was the most delightful thing imaginable. Alibech answered that she had heard so. He further told her that it consisted in putting the Devil into Hell. The juvenile Mahometan readily swallowed this, for she had been taught that the Devil was God's mortal enemy.

Her zeal and curiosity were now aroused to the highest pitch, and she requested Rusticus to show her the soul saving process without further delay.

The hermit did not wait to be asked a second time.

"Follow my example," he said, taking off his clothes, and kneeling down before her in the attitude of prayer. The tone and manner of the hypocrite were so devout, that Alibech was completely overpowered, and obeyed unhesitatingly.

"Now place yourself close up in front of me," said the holy father.

As the innocent Alibech obeyed, she perceived that something attached to Rusticus was exercising in a manner most wonderful.

"What is that?" she exclaimed, all astonishment.

"My child," impatiently answered the hermit, "that is the Devil by which I am beset, and unless you assist me to put him into Hell, I believe I shall die instantly; so excrutiating are the torments to which he is subjecting me."

As Alibech had been taught that the Devil beset

almost everybody, the mere fact of his fastening upon the hermit, did not surprise her. *   *

The first lessons in Christianism, as taught by St. Rusticus, were very painful to so young a girl as Alibech. But the pious exhortations of her holy accomplice kept her spirits up, and she finally acknowledged that putting the Devil into Hell was more pleasant than anything else she had ever experienced; besides, it had the advantage of saving two souls at once.

In spite of the hypocritical affectation of the old fogies, I percieved that their abnormal tastes were highly gratified by this tale ; at the same time there was no mistaking the disgust which all the rest of the company manifested for the deep hypocrisy, heartless treachery, and all but "total depravity," that prevailed in the *Moral* ages.

"If the fear of 'Hell' had been wholly out of the question, " observed one of the gentlemen, "I don't see how that hypocritical old Christian, Rusticus, could bear the thoughts of doing what he did, well knowing, that, as mankind were then situated, it would be pretty sure to bring disgrace and ruin on an innocent young girl."

The parson, in a very mild and subdued tone, ventured to remark that Rusticus was a Catholic, and didn't deserve the name of Christian ; that Gibbon was a prejudiced infidel, and Boccaccio only a mere story-teller.

"Well," said I, " but Lot and his daughters were not Catholics, nor in your estimation was the account of *their* actions, written by an infidel, or a mere story-teller; yet those actions were incomparably more abominable than those of Alibech and Rusticus, and their narrator leaves it to be fairly inferred that 'God' sanctioned them. Moreover, the story of Lot and his daughters is utterly void of literary merit: it is unmitigated bawdiness and most horrible blasphemy. Yet Protestants spent an incalculable amount of money in supplying innocent young men and women with the book that contained that story, and many others almost as nasty."

"Why is it that there are now three or four women to one man?" asked the political economist.

"Because natural supply is necessarily adequate to demand," answered the Grand Artist. "Foolish, short-sighted old fogyism long obstructed the operation of this law, but it could not always do so. Nature is at last disenthralled; all her resources are brought into play, and both ends meet, as the saying used to be; and she makes just so many women more than men and has through her crowning method, art, placed the sexual relations on such a footing, that it is not *necessary* for men to violate their strongest feelings and forego their most positive rights, nor for women to gratify such feelings and grant such rights, when to do so would entail on themselves long years of loathsome and most painful disease, nor when it would inflict slow murder on their unborn progeny. Women abhor sexual connection with men during the catamenial flow; they had to be abnormally urged to it, after the first months of pregnancy; and it generally produced the loathsome *whites*, and the terrible woes of *prolapsus uteri*, if their husbands cohabited with them within six weeks after childbirth.

"And now, gentlemen, (addressing all the old fogies) I ask, did you not violate your wives in some, if not all of these respects, and with results quite as dreadful as those I have described?"

Notwithstanding this home-thrust at the so-called marriage institution, the poor old fogies hung down their heads in profound silence.

"Sexual intercourse at any time during lactation was most repugnant to woman, and highly injurious both to her and the child," continued the Grand Artist. "And now, gentlemen, I will put one more question in consideration of the many you have put to me, and you may answer it at your leisure, as it will require some calculation. If you had *monogamically* married your stallions to your mares, and your bulls to your cows, how much would your colts and calves have been worth? or, if you had sowed the same seed on the same ground year after year, how long would your crops have been worth gathering? *Nature abhors nothing so much as sameness! and that abhorrence is intense or passive in proportion to highness or lowness in the scale of being. Be sure you take this into your calculation*, and don't forget that what nature most intensely abhors, she *necessarily and inevitably most severely punishes.*"

"Mankind have never been such fools as to suppose that any part of nature except themselves could thrive in that covert of bawdiness—that hotbed of crime, vice, disease, and all that is foul and morbific—that condition most falsely named marriage. There never was a pure, inviolate '*legal*' marriage; *almost* every such marriage was a continual adultery, according to the rule laid down by the very authority from whence it claimed to be derived. Almost every 'married' man and woman did lust after others' with a perfect looseness; the very purest of *moral* men and women did *sometimes* thus 'commit adultery' and render their marriage contract null and void *theoretically*, and the most degrading of possible connections, in consequence of not being nullified *practically*.

"As you have so little to do," asked the persistent moralist, "pray how do you spend your time so as to keep out of that debasement into which *too much material prosperity* plunged the upper classes of the society to which we belonged?"

"Your question is such a vexatious jumble," answered his Highness, "that it will take much time and more patience to unravel it, for a clear answer. In the first place, your 'too much material prosperity' consisted in a surplus of 'money' or property valued by the money standard (instead of by its *actual* worth) with a dreadful scantiness of pleasant means for spending it. And almost the only competition among *your* upper classes was for the possession of this so-called 'money,' and this delusive wealth, or to outdo each other in ever-changing fashion, and in vexatious, ridiculous, and unsatisfactory show. To 'kill time,' therefore, *your* upper classes crammed their stomachs with unwholesome food, generally at most unseasonable hours, besotted their brains with liquors more or less abominable, and stupefied themselves, and brought swift destruction on what little health and beauty they possessed, by chewing, smoking, and snuffing just the nastiest weed to be found in the vegetable kingdom. The richest men, and the most royal princes stupefied themselves, during a great portion of their time, *substantially* to a level with the dirtiest beggars that could afford to suck a tobacco pipe. The 'rich' who could not endure life thus, and by varying its monotony by an occasional sea voyage, and a good clearing out spell of sea sickness, had recourse to gambling, to seducing their neighbour's wives, to debauching their own servant girls, and committing rape on their slaves. And vast numbers of them contracted a taste altogether too nasty to be mentioned except in medical works or 'Holy Writ.'" (See Romans I., 26, 27).

"Suppose," said one of the ladies, "we show our visitors how rich people now employ their time; and let that answer their question."

We now took the old fogies into the work shops, all of which were perfectly free from dust, smoke, and everything annoying or unhealthy, and where little else was necessary to be done except the delightful task of tending and beholding the machinery. There, they saw, at a glance, that although wealth was incomparably more individualized than they ever knew it to be, it created very little rivalry on its own account; just enough to preserve the *meum* and *tuam* in the case. Men and women prided themselves almost wholly on their skill and agility in what little there was to do. There was no department of labor wherein the richest capitalists were not to be seen competing for this prize as earnestly as did those who were the smallest stockholders in the world's great company. No one who is even slightly acquainted with history and common affairs will wonder at this, for it is a well known fact that some Roman Emperors prided themselves chiefly on their skill as equestrians in a dirty circus; and that some English peers have taken more satisfaction in being gazetted for their adroitness in stage driving, than in contemplating their patent of nobility. Does any one doubt that Lord Stanhope was prouder of his improvements in stereotyping than of his nobility? or that Prince Albert was as jealous of his honour as a good agriculturist, and *a powerful chief in the World's Fair*, as of his fame in being the husband of Queen Victoria? See, too, how this principle works even in that most fatiguing of all occupations,—dragging and pumping fire engines; to excel even in this, men who are pretty well off sometimes quit their warm beds during the coldest and stormiest nights of winter.

We now took the old fogies to several agricultural scenes truly heavenly, and then to a silvery lake, at a short distance, where hundreds of ladies and gentlemen were, in all their naked charmingness, competing with each other at swimming. Hard by, a company of equestrians of both sexes, mounted on mares and stallions, far superior to the geldings of former times, (cruelty, even to animals, being now abolished,) were performing feats which threw all the circuses of the olden time into the shade.

"I suppose you have glorious fun at skating and sleigh riding in Winter time, don't you?" asked the parson.

"People once tried to extract fun out of skating and sleigh riding, and the parsons encouraged them to do so, to keep them away from balls and theatres," said the grand Artist, "but the world has pretty much done with ice and snow; water seldom freezes even at the north pole in January. We will treat you to a ride there in a balloon car, one of these days. You'll then see the most gorgeous twilight you ever beheld."

"Is it possible? Who would have thought it?' exclaimed all the old fogies.

"It was thought possible long before it came to pass!" said I. "Charles Fourier had a glorious foresight of it, and the author of Vestiges of Creation gave a strong hint that he thought it would come to pass. And, following these hints, together with those of Oken, and basing himself firmly on the materialism of Aguste Comte and Ludwig Feuerbach, the announcer of '*The Religion of Science*' demonstrated not only the possibility, but the absolute certainty of just such a state of things as now exists throughout the entire world. Following a suggestion of Hamboldt, and critically examining the thermometrical tables kept at various parts of the world, he proved that thermal phenomena do not depend a tenth part so much as physicists and astronomers supposed, on the obliqueness or perpendicularity of the solar rays; he called attention to the fact that every year there were, in any given latitude, days in February and July, in which the temperature was *nearly or quite the same*.. As to luminous phenomena, there are numerous instances on record of their utter inexplicability on old theories. All thermality and luminosity necessary to man are *producible, and have been produced*, in and on the earth; in its atmosphere, and in proximate ether.

They are intimately connected with electric phenomena, and *sufficiently controllable by man*. The lightning conductor and magnetic telegraph were only the rudiments of electro-dynamics.

Logically, also, the thing was self evident to people capable of generally comprehending the great whole which the subject involved.

Our senses, being but functions of materialness, cannot cognize beyond the bounds of material existence. They can, indeed, commit most absurd errors in arranging, connecting, and locating their cognizances; such, only, were the errors of the so-called "supernatural" conception. Heaven *was*, simply, the most unscientific and bungling preconception that ignorance could form of *earthly* perfection.

That man desires perfection, is self-evident. If, then, perfection is not attainable *in* nature, then, and in that case. desire, aye, and conception, too, evidently extends *out of nature*, and the supernatural stands proven. But all talk about supernaturalness is mere balderdash.

But let no one of you pretend that perfection is, or can be desired except through material means—except through *the requisite human exertion*. If it could be had miraculously—for the mere asking—it would pall on the appetite as soon as tasted. No-one wants perfection in that way; they who say they do, simply don't know what they are gabbling about."

"Why was not this great discovery—*the Religion of Science*—acted on instantly?" asked the unbe liever. " Why was it not put in practice right off, like the steam-engine ?"

"The steam-engine was a *simple* contrivance that everybody could *minutely* understand, and out of which *any* one could see that *money could readily be made*. But the system in question is even now *minutely* understood only by a very few. The masses *feel* it to be true, and all right as the children in school have told you. People might have saved themselves inexpressible woes by withdrawing their confidence from mysteryites, moralists, skeptics, and demagogues, and bestowing it on the scientists and artists sooner than they did."

At the period when the "*Religion of Science*" was announced, labor saving machinery was so far developed, that with less than three hours *productive* labor per day, by all able men and women, everybody could have lived almost as magnificently and a thousand times more happily than did the most fortunate princes or the luckiest demagogues. But they who invented the machines and they who furnished the capital to put them into action, attempted to run them for their own exclusive benefit. They hadn't comprehension enough to ask themselves—" If we throw half the people out of work, or into duplicate, or unnecessary labor, such as *free traders*, from five hundred to ten thousand miles asunder, and carriers for such *free trade*, and if we compel the other half of the people to work for just wages enough to keep soul and body together, after the most wretched fashion, where are our customers to come from? who will buy the products of our machines? And when they piled up ready made clothing and cutlery, in their warehouses, till all had to be tumbled into auction to pay for the raw material, and didn't bring half enough to pay even that much, the political economists told them they had been *over producing!* Yes, *over producing!* when, staring them in the face, or clamoring fearfully, an eighth part of "the people" were in absolute squalor; shivering, for want of a coat, or a pair of shoes, and vainly begging for work whereby to earn them!! When every twentieth woman was prostituting herself for clothing or shelter!!! and when all the rest who could, sold themselves for life for the same purpose!!!!"

"But suppose we had shared our capital, and the product of our machines, *in common* with everybody? is it not evident that all effort would come to a dead stand still?" asked the capitalists and machinists.

"True," said the announcer of the Religion of Science," but suppose that, instead of doing the next foolish thing to the one you *are* doing, you share your capital and sl ill with the laborers, who *make it available*, to just the extent that will make you as rich as you *really* can be—incomparably richer than you now are, and at the same time furnish just the *individual stimulus* that shall induce the laborers to provide themselves *and you* with all that they *and you* want?"

Fourier made far greater discoveries than any other man, considering when he lived. It was from a stand point furnished by Fourier, Comte, and Feuerbach, that the announcer of the Religion of Science was enabled to foresee and prove that "Heaven could be *fully* and *to all intents and purposes*, realized on Earth, without recourse to "beyond the skies," without going outside of time and sense!"

When the hour for rest came, as the old fogies retired to their "homestead," their looks clung, as if fixed to the ravishing beauties who, with most bewitching coquetry, were playing with the gentlemen at the game of *partners for the night.*

"Can't some of us take pity on these miserable creatures?" said one of the ladies with tears glistening in her diamond eyes, that had never before been thus moistened.

"Don't think of such a thing," said a physiologist who was present. "Nobody in the *moral* ages, was free from every one of the thousand chronic forms the venereal and scrofulous diseases took on; and the *mildest* of these forms of disease would virulently affect such pure constitutions as you possess."*

"I hope you didn't think me in earnest," said the lady. "I only gave way, or rather my tongue did, to a sudden gush of pity. I don't believe I could have to do sexually with the least ugly of these wretches, without such violence to my nature as would prove fatal to me."

---

* In the Sandwich Islands, where free love prevailed, the venereal disease was unknown, till it was imported thither from monogamous countries. That disease was produced by the system which acknowledged prostitution to be one of its "necessary evils." The *moral* doctors admitted that the *greatest evils* were beyond the cure of the *best remedies* they knew of.

PART THIRD.

THE OLD WAY AND THE NEW WAY SPICILY CONTRASTED.

Next day was the Anniversary of the Final Downfall of Mysticism and Humbug. A vast concourse of people from all parts of the world had come to celebrate it; to accommodate them, a table several miles in circumference was set in the open air.

After breakfast the Grand Artist conducted me to a seat in his balloon car; and now, I perceived that our festive board was completely surrounded by these aerial conveyances. In a few minutes, the whole vast company were seated in them, and the signal was given to ascend. These cars, you must understand, were just as manageable as birds on the wing. At a height sufficient to clear the trees and palace domes, we extended the circle the cars formed, till, from every point of the horizon, they displayed the very sublimity of magnificence. A rise about three times higher next took place.

The Grand Artist's car now broke from the ring, and took the centre. A general waving of flags, by the ladies, and a universal " *all hail*" from the gentlemen, accompanied this splendid movement, which signified that power and might were now immutably concentrated for liberty, instead of for either king or demagogue oppression.

His Highness, with our assistance, now unfurled a large and most splendid banner, with this inscription:— "HUMANITY IS GOD: EARTH IS HEAVEN: LIBERTY IS REAL." Simultaneously there dropped from every car a beautiful parachute, with a streamer bearing the same glorious inscription.

All the cars in the ring now started off in elliptical orbits, around the grand center of freedom-power, and, to cap the climax of this magnificent representation of the solar system, (after which the social system was now remodelled) the two cars at the eastern and western extremities of the circle took *very* elliptical orbits, outside of all the others, and unfolded long, glittering streamers, or tails, which gave the appearance of comets.

Our car now led off, followed by the others, in a series of evolutions the most pleasing and wonderful that can be imagined, till, the hour for dinner having arrived, we all came to anchor precisely on that part of *terra firma* where we started from.

For about two hours we gave ourselves up to feasting, friendship, and the most hilarious mirth. The wine flowed with perfect freedom; not a particle did it impede our liberty; for not one of us got drunk, though all of us drank just as much as we pleased. A complete system of physical education had made the tastes and appetites of all, unerring guides as to what was good and sufficient. The ladies and gentlemen almost simultaneously left the table, first to enjoy a promenade, and then a *siesta*, in the flowery groves; lounges and hammocks being everywhere provided for that purpose. After which, and while preparations were making for the evening's entertainments, the Grand Artist took me to view the monuments. These were very numerous, and all in the most admirable taste. They were all erected to general or special scientists and artists; such men as Locke, Bacon, Galileo, Harvey, Bichat, Columbus, Newton, Laplace, Fulton, Daguere, Faust, Morse, Guido, Titian, Power, Ling, Gall, Priessnitz, Euclid, Lagrange, Sir Humphry Davy, Broussais, William Lawrence, Owen, Fourier, Comte, Buckle, and one that modesty forbids me to name, were among the immortals. But few ladies who belonged to the Dismal Ages were in the list, though after the *Good Time* came, more than one-third of the monuments were to women who had distinguished themselves principally in the finer arts. Not one of all these monuments bore the name of any one who had beem conspicuous as a mysteryite, moralist, king, emperor, or demagogue; the little, narrow, spiteful systems had all "had their day, and ceased to be;" the pages of very musty books, which very curious people sometimes glanced at, in pity and disgust, contained all that was left of those systems and their inventors.

"In '1860' the announcer of "*The Religion of Science*" warned these wretches of their fate, and that warning has been preserved on this table of stone; read it," said the Grand Artist. It read as follows:—

"Moralists, Mysteryites, and Politicians! If your

cowardly, *double-faced hypocrisy* was not *suicidally blinding*, you would see that your proper function—your *real* interest—is to *abolish* constraint : not to impose and perpetuate it. If you knew with what abhorrence you will be remembered in *the good time coming*, you would gladly barter your immortality, even, for an exchange of places, on the record, with those you term the 'vilest of the vile.' But there is *one* way, and one *only*, whereby you can somewhat mitigate that abhorrence. Clothe yourselves in sack-cloth black as night, and nasty as the rag-picker can furnish. Down on your knees in the filthiest streets and lanes of the world's cities, bury your faces deep in the dust and mud thereof, and implore the murderers, thieves, harlots and beggars who there inhabit, to pardon you. Acknowledge, in terms as supplicating and humble as possible, that your impostures and crimes are unsurpassable ; that *your* guilt is the sum of *all* guilt ; that you deserve 'eternal damnation' infinitely more than do any creatures who wear the human form. Beg hard on the score of ignorance. You can make a strong point there. In fact, *that's your only hope*."

"This singular *bronze* statue, in the shape of a tree, with very luxuriant foliage, and with no inscription that I can see ;—what's the meaning of it ?" I asked.

"Open the leaves that cluster so thickly where the fruit ought to grow," said the Grand Artist.

I did so, and found nothing inside but a most provoking emptiness.

"Now, critically examine the trunk," said His Highness.

I did so; and after a good deal of hunting, found the name of H..... t S..... r.

"Quite appropriate," I remarked; "this H.....t S..... r wrote some *very* good things; his phrases raised great expectations in myself and other social architects; but we got as sorely disappointed, by the time we read through his essays, as I have been in trying to discover, by its fruit, what sort of a tree the curious monument that perpetuates his memory represents. The man took especial pains to abjure Comte, and he was never even suspected of following Kant. Nor did he evince a clear preference for any of the infinitessimal differences between Comte and Kant. He described popular government as the most clumsy and awkward of social systems, yet capable of doing *all that ought to be done!* Hobbe's '*Leviathan*' infused into him a vague conception of the 'Social Organism,' but his political belief, as near as it could be made out, seemed to be, that, somehow or other, mankind would come to frown as contemptuously on those, who, by fraud in trade or politics, obtained money by millions, as they did on those who picked pockets or robbed hen-roosts; that frown was the nostrum that would purify the body politic; but he no more told how that frown could be fixed on the popular face, than the mice in council determined *how* to get the bell on the cat. H.....t S..... r didn't take it into his calculation, that, in spite of all the frowning that could be got up, there would be plenty of big thieves to keep each other in countenance, so long as government itself was a 'necessary evil'—a monster brigand which society tolerated in hopes of thereby escaping the inflictions of a more *irregular* brigandage."

"And what mean these queer looking monuments, bottom upwards, and surmounted by snakes, monkeys, and asses' heads?" I asked.

"These," replied the Grand Artist, "commemorate the shame and keep up the disgrace of those cowardly, and sneaking thieves who tried to steal the fame of others. These miserable poltroons were time-servers; they had understanding enough to see the fallaciousness of the social mysticism and moralism they flattered for bread and butter and the multitude's applause, and they didn't relish the scorn which they could plainly see all sensible people held them in. So they preached, lectured, conversed, and wrote, *all in a double sense;* one sense for the many, the other sense for the few. By means of *throwing out feelers*, they discovered when the time was ripe for putting forth *as their own*, plans of reform, the originators of which, they had *done their best to smother*. They often temporarily succeeded; but my predecessors spared no pains in pointing out their contemptible scoundrelism, and in making a just record of it. Some of these reversed monuments, you perceive, are erected to those who strove to eclipse the man, who, assisted by Comte and Fourier, *as he gratefully acknowledged*, presignificantly announced the perfection which now everywhere prevails. These reversed monuments *seem*, at first sight, to show vindictiveness; but their *real* significancy is only justice. They chiefly excite *pity* for those named thereon."

My attention was so taken up with these monuments, that the announcement of supper quite surprised me.

On this occasion, supper was almost as substantial as dinner had been; for it preceded the Ball that was to wind up the grand celebration, instead of being jammed into the middle of it, as ball-suppers were during the ages when everything was topsy turvy.

As soon as it was quite dark, every palace, that is to say every dwelling in the capitol was brilliantly illuminated, and the walls of their saloons were hung round with the glorious banners that had been detached from the parachutes aforementioned.

Carpeted alleys, on this occasion, connected all the palaces with each other, practically turning their saloons into one.

Amidst all the enchantment that the combined power of mankind and all in the connection could produce, "music arose, with its voluptuous swell,' "soft eyes look'd love to eyes which spake again," and all was joy and merriment in the highest; for this was the anniversary of *the only lawful, true, self-sustaining, and therefore indissoluble marriage of all man and womankind, present and prospective:*—the anniversary of the final downfall of Hell and Humbug, and the inauguration of perfect and univeral bliss.

On this glorious occasion, the wedding of several hundred young ladies and gentlemen,—their initiation into the closest and most delightful connection with universal humanity—took place. The ceremony was even more beautiful and interesting than anything I had yet seen. I observed that the neophytes in the rites and mysteries of Venus, did not choose to be initiated by each other, but by the *ripest and most voluptuous adepts;* who, in many instances, were two or three times older than themselves; and these adepts did not refuse to perform the sweet office, you may be perfectly sure. *En passant*, reader, don't forget that the people I am telling you about, did not look so old at two hundred years, as you do, if you are a woman of thirty, or a man of fifty.

But the old fogies were persuaded to go to the theater that night, the plays having been arranged for their special edification.

The evening's entertainments commenced with the serio-ludicrous farce, called

MORAL TRANSMUTATION.

OR THE

MAGICAL FLIP-FLAPS AND ASTONISHING SUMMERSAULTS

PERFORMED UNDER

THE GREAT IMPOSSIBLENESS.

PROGRAMME.

Council of State in the olden time.—Enter the Chief. He lays down the rules of government. Justice and right must be *enforced.* "Moral Principle" must be the rule of action. Every man and every woman must reform himself or herself, and do as they would be done by.

Enter a Policeman.—I have arrested a thief. I caught him stealing *twenty dollars!*

Chief Justice.—Put him on the treadmill as long as he can bear it; give him thirty days solitary confinement on bread and water; make him hammer stone, or perform some other labor equally hard.—Insult and disgrace him all you possibly can.—Whip him severely, or almost drown him, as often as you can get up the slightest excuse for so doing. At night, closely encase him between cold, damp stone walls, with so little bed-clothes that he will be in a constant shiver. If he survives this treatment three years, let him be disfranchised and turned loose on the public.

Enter another policeman.—I have arrested a murderer.

Chief Justice.—Give him time to say his prayers, then hang him by the neck till he is dead, and may God have mercy on his soul!

Enter a Messenger, in hot haste.—Oh, there's such an awful big lot of thieves and murderers got together, stealing all they can, and murdering all who oppose them! We've captured a few of them, but they've carried off some of our folks; and they swear that, if we resort to hanging and imprisoning in *their* case, we shall speedily find out that two can play at that game. They've seized a big slice of our territory, with its cities, arsenals, forts, prisons, and people. They've set up a government of their own, and assume to have as good right to enact law, and enforce moral principle as we have.

Chief.—What! Thieves and murderers enact law? **Brigands set up on moral principle? I should'n't** wonder if the scoundrels established churches next, and invoked the blessing of Almighty God on their rascality.

Messenger.—Oh! they've done that already.—Thousands of clergymen are preaching in their favor from texts in our own Bible, and praying for them as devoutly as they once did for us. Their parsons and ours are praying a regular sweepstakes against each other for a wager, from appearances. And their fast day proclamation. (handing a newspaper.) It's as full of piety as any of our own ever were.

Chaplain.—Speak more reverently of the clergy, sir, if you please, and don't make light of prayer.

Enter an Emissary with propositions from the wholesale Thieves and Murderers.

Chief.—Guards, take him out and shoot him instantly! Hold! that won't do, though! Villain! our military will settle this business with your infamous gang! Begone!

The Battle Field. Fearful slaughter. The thieves and murderers gain the advantage.

Head Quarters of the Thieves and Murderers. Enter plenipotentiaries with a treaty of peace. They and the head thieves and murderers sign it. The latter acknowledged as *rulers, fully entitled to the* PRAYERS *of the* "*Church,*" *and the admiration and* "MORAL" SUPPORT *of mankind.*

Nemesis of "*Moral Principle.*" The old and new nation hold a jubilee over one more brute force transmutation of wrong to right. All the governments and peoples in the world fraternise with the late thieves and murderers, and call them *good and honorable men ;* thus *practically* acknowledging that they despise and punish crime only for its being perpetrated on a contemptibly small scale, and that they are ever ready to reward rascality so soon as it achieves success. *All the " Churches"* sanction this proceeding. The "infidels" consider it " necessary" to the maintenance of "civil government." They haven't the brains to inquire—then *what's the use of " civil government?"*

The little, unfortunate villians confined in prisons, and those under sentence of death, take courage, on hearing of the wonderful elasticity of "justice," (?) and ask to be at least pardoned; but they are summarily told that their request is in contempt of "law," (?) subversive of "religion" (?) and utterly at variance with "moral principle."

The manager informed the audience that this farce had been substantially played in good earnest, over and over and over again, there was no telling how many times, before mankind discovered that "moral principle" was the " angel of darkness" transformed to an "angel of light." It *created* malice and *offered premiums* on atrociousness while *seeming* to be *immaculate right itself.* It was the make-shift of incapacity. It was the lowest spawn of ignorance, that father of all evil. It was the quackery of quackeries and masked hellishness which set man at war with nature, imposed Church Atheism, inflicted State Anarchy, and whelmed the world in violence and woe.

In a notable instance, under the regime of "moral principle," a gang of thieves and murderers who caused the death of eight or nine hundred thousand people, and stole or destroyed at least ten thousand million dollars worth of property, were pardoned, and restored to " honourable" citizenship, with the exception of a few ringleaders; most of these got clear under the subterfuge of prisoners of war; and all the others escaped, richly laden with booty, and were received by the most Christian and " moral" nations in the world, with coldness 'tis true, on account of their failure in iniquity, but not with anything like the contempt that small villians met with in those nations.

When these brigands and murderers were in the flood tide of their success, the Pope called their chief " Most Illustrious President;" and the *divinity* students of Oxford gave that chief three heartier cheers than they ever before bestowed on a foreigner. In this instance, too, when the pardoning time came, the little unfortunate rogues claimed pardon, but were refused, because, in point of *fact and plain truth*, their crimes were not great and atrocious enough to excite the respect and admiration of *moral principled mankind*.

Judges who, when legislators, had violated their official oath, and stealthily pocketed fifty or a hundred thousand dollars to vote for the most unjust and extortionate laws, sentenced people to fine and imprisonment for selling beer on Sunday!

Such knavery as stealing a loaf of bread, to prevent starvation, was the lowest disgrace, under the "Moral Principle" regime; a robbery, accompanied by murder, was not considered half so contemptible. Ten thousand robberies and murders entitled the perpetrators thereof to " THE RIGHTS OF BELLIGErants," by *common consent of all Christendom!*

These rights included the privilege of selling piratical plunder to merchants belonging to the most respectable and "orthodox" Christian churches! men, too, whose "moral principle" it would be libellous to question!

And the chief robbers and murderers were treated with the respect accorded to rulers, by every government but the one they were fighting with; and even that government treated them with the respect they showed to military chiefs.

And so "Moral Principle" went on till it crushed to death under the weight of its own damnableness.

As the manager finished this epilogue, two automatons, in Dismal Age costumes, jumped on the stage, and with a regular old fashioned fife and drum, performed an ear-splitting medley, called "Folly's Rampage;" it was composed of "Yankee Doodle," the "Army and Navy Forever," and several other "fought, bled and died" tunes.

The laughter quickly subsided, and now came the grand spectacle of the evening. It was entitled

CREATION.
PROGRAMME.

ACT I.

The boundless expanse of etherialness; giving the nearest possible idea of ante-time, ante-space, ante-duration, and the absolute nothing, which super-sensible people declare must necessarily have preceded intelligible existence. Perceptibility takes place at the center of vision. This perceptibility revolves; and, around it, the universal etherialness condenses into discernible objectivity, following the motion of the first discernibleness, till all within the circle of vision becomes a whirling mass, less and less opaque from the center to a *seeming* verge, where a ring forms, and the connection with surrounding universalness *apparently* breaks off. As the great ball condenses, the ring bursts, throwing off fragments which also become rotating balls; then the ring re-forms and throws off other such balls; and so on to the number of planets in the Solar System; these planets, meantime, throwing off their satellites or moons.

ACT II.

The Earth presented to view as a ball of fire. It cools from the poles to the equator, forming a granite crust, upheaved at short intervals, by the boiling lava underneath. Countless ages are supposed to pass away, and soil is formed; the volcanic action having become greatly lessened. Other countless ages, and the primary Flora appears; the volcanoes being still more reduced in number. Other countless ages, and the lower Fauna is developed. Other countless ages, and mankind are *rudimentally* "created."

ACT III.

Human ignorance and human destitution as complete as possible. Mankind finding themselves endowed with *all but* infinitely more desire than they know how to satisfy in this material world during life, postpone *nearly* all happiness, to be enjoyed in a " spiritual," and confessedly *unintelligible* world, *after death !* They set about *repressing* their instincts, except those on the gratification of which bare existence depends. Confucius, Plato, and other " moral" compromisers with evil, arise. All their machinations against omnipotent nature perfectly unavailing, and more and more disastrous.— Still their fooleries are allowed to constitute the basis of " religion" and " government," and material art, to which " civilization" was indebted for all its advantages over savagery, and by which perfection was at last achieved, has to fight its way against these fooleries, and be subordinate to them.

ACT IV.

Advent of " The Messiah." Fire and brimstone " peace on earth and good will to men." Plato's non-sensuous *post-mortem* " Heaven" adopted. How the scheme worked. The fire and brimstone peacemakers take the name of " Christians," and attempt to undermine Paganism. The Pagans retaliate.— Dreadful slaughter. Fire and brimstone victorious.

ACT V.

Advent of Mohammed. He pitches into the fire and brimstone peace-makers with their own weapons, and holds out the lure of a post-mortem *sensuous* " Heaven." Wonderful success. The Crusades.

Unprecedented human slaughter. Mohammed comes within a hair's breadth of exterminating "The Messiah's" "religion."

ACT VI.

Galileo reveals the solar system. Columbus discovers America. Mosaic Astronomy and Christian Geography upset. Consternation and fury of the priesthood. Horrors of the Inquisition. The "Reformation." "Moral" opposition to the laws according to which almightiness constituted human nature, carried on with unprecedented vigour. Abominable consequences. *The Venereal Disease makes its appearance.*

ACT VII.

The Christians rapaciously grab the "New World." The Protestant Christians set about exterminating the North American Indians and appropriating their lands. The Catholic Christians seize the vast wealth of the Peruvians and Mexicans, and slaughter or enslave its owners. The Protestant Christians, unable to make slaves of their American victims, who prefer death to bondage, butcher fourteen millions of them, and meanwhile inaugurate the African slave trade. Unsurpassable cruelties perpetrated on board the Christian slave-ships.

ACT VIII.

Most of the Colonies planted by "Christian" and "moral" England in North America revolt, and set up the "Model Republic." "Declaration of Independence." All men declared rightfully entitled to life, liberty, and the "*pursuit*" of happiness. Underhand reservation with respect to Indians and Negroes. Thomas Paine defines the rights of man from the theo-moral stand-point, prudently blinking over the Indian and Negro questions for the time being, on the ground that "error may safely be trusted where *reason* is left free to combat it;" and very consistently, *under the circumstances*, counselling violence in obtaining human rights. Washington also, under pressure of instant necessity, acquiesces, and consents to be military chief, and afterwards President. "*Rotation in office.*" The nation's treasury to be raffled for every four years under the specious guise of a "*Presidential Election.*" Washington resigns, to see if the new ship of state can keep any time from going to wreck without having him for pilot.

ACT IX

Charles Fourier discovers the great system of co-operative labor, capital, skill, and the human passions. Auguste Comte gives super-materialism its death-blow. Calvin Blanchard announces the Religion of Science and Government in accordance therewith.

ACT X.

View of the "United States." The largest and finest country in the world, and gratuitously furnished with all the "Old World" science and art. No other government ever commenced under anything near such favourable auspices. Things go on "bunkum," till demagoguery becomes rampant.— Douglass, hell-bent on the Presidency, resolves to put "elective franchise" to its utmost stretch. Majority-force is highest law and highest religion. It sanctifies slavery, rape, and murder. Supreme-court Judges mere political weather-cocks to "decide" which way demagogue-instigated popular wrong and foolishness rushes. "To the victors belong the spoils." The weak (*lyingly*, in a vast number of instances, called Negroes, or blacks) have no rights which the strong are bound to respect." The Republic's first principles appealed to. The political gospel of Calhoun in the ascendant. "Government justly derives its authority only from the consent [*and implied wisdom*] of the governed," or rather a majority of the governed; Indians, and Negroes, and slaves no matter how white, being always considered as of no consequence. Secession logically results. Jeff. Davis and Co. draw the sword in vindication of the "Constitutional" right of the United States to go all to pieces and split into an indefinite number of contemptible little demagogueries. Vallandigham, Wood, Seymour, and their crew, surreptitiously or ignorantly back up Jeff. Davis and Co., with the "Constitution" in one hand, and the other apparently ready to seize the sword as soon as they dare, and plunge that sword to the hilt in the vitals of the "Model Republic." France and England, like vultures hovering over a dying elephant, eagerly watch for the "Model Republic's" dissolution. France seizes Mexico, a Republic already gone to seed. Jeff. Davis and his Confederate fiends cause the southern unionists to be torn to pieces by blood-hounds, as only slaves had formerly been. Union prisoners hanged, whipped, branded, sold to slavery, and starved to death by thousands. Seymour's New York "friends" burn orphan asylums, roast people in the streets, and try to reduce the whole city to ashes. "Hell" inaugurated on earth. Christians sink so far below wolves, tigers, or *any other beasts*, that they *generally* encourage, or look complacently on the pummelling of each other to death for *mere sport!* Prize-fighting championship between the two leading Christian and "moral" nations. Bullyism holds the balance of power at the so-called "elections." Corruption goes it so strong as to make it perfectly evident that if the state prisons and legislative halls changed inmates, the public would be greatly benefitted thereby!— The "Church" cants about "vice" and "crime," knowing that she derives a great portion of her support from gamblers, the rent and even *direct* proceeds of brothels, and fraudulent debtors; and the entire balance from a system that degrades all labor to performance by whip-dreading Negroes, or starvation-impelled white slaves :—the latter, in a multitude of instances, actually worked *and* starved to death! Even *common* thieves and swindlers are numbered by tens of thousands in all the great cities of Christendom, and their yearly (in some places monthly) plunder is reckoned by millions.— Inside view of Pandemonium, exhibiting the most " devilish" failure and " hellish" summing up of countless ages of moralism, nineteen centuries of Christianism, an incalculable amount of skepticism, and eighty five years of caucus and ballot-boxism.

ACT XI.

Utopia's last revival. Caucus and ballotboxism reduced to the lowest state of humiliation. The "Model Republic," gasping for life, courts the alliance of the most absolute despotism in the world, thus completely crushing out the republican hopes of down trodden Poland. But the "elective franchise" swindle, or demagogue pest nevertheless extends over all Europe. One more patch up of it in America. Worse and worse. The " Connecticut Blue Laws" revived all over the United States. The American Congress outcants the famous " Praise-God-Barebones-Parliament" of England. Newspaper editors submit to the lowest humiliation in their necessity to please the taste of their " moral principle" befooled patrons.

Mankind will learn only in the very dearest school kept by that most expensive teacher, experience; they seem determined to go to "Heaven" via " Hell." The selected wisdom of a country with idle means enough to profitably employ all the muscle in the world, starts a project for transporting four million laborers on account of their colour! Unprecedented multitudes of prostitutes. Six hundred thousand discharged soldiers clamour for some thing to do whereby to obtain bread for themselves and their starving families, and a government with millions on millions of acres of rich wild land, and boundless untouched mineral resources, *don't know* how to organize industry, and employ these discharged soldiers! A petition, written by one man [the author of the Religion of Science] who *does know*, and signed by a few others who approve the measure, is sent to Congress, asking an appropriation for a National Joint Stock Organization of Labor, Capital, and Skill, to cultivate these lands, and work these mines by these discharged soldiers, and provide employment and a suitable home for the prostitutes. The petition treated with contempt, as being for something " unconstitutional," " utopian," and in danger of resulting in failure! The head petitioner tells Congress that, Constitution or no Constitution, they *must* organize the said Company, and vote $1,000,000,000 therefor, or else continue periodically to vote two or three thousand millions to slaughter human beings, and do at least ten thousand millions damage besides. But the "public servants" nevertheless cling to the Constitution, and tne damnable foolery connected therewith. The parsons, politicians, and moralists, would roast the petitioners alive, but for their own mutual distrusts and jealousies. Compulsion, compulsion, compulsion! Nothing could gain a hearing but compulsion!! Capitalists and inventors, blind as Congressmen, invest fabulous amounts in fancy stock concerns that daily collapse like soap bubbles, and let millions of people prey on them as idlers, robbers, destroyers, and legal or illegal harlots, rather than take them into partnership as wealth producers! they, too, sneer at "utopias," and oppose a change of measures *for fear of failure!* as if there could possibly be any worse failure than the perpetual failure that had been going on ever since "the beginning." Christianized, civilized, and everlastingly moralized England, treats her laboring people worse than she treats her horses, her cattle, or her hogs. She puts women in harness in collieries, *where mules would die too fast and cost too much!* Government makes a hullabalo over a single murder by a single individual, yet no Christian government long abstains from perpetrating ten thousand or a million cold blooded murders! Christians kill each other at the rate of millions a month; and Christian rulers and priests appoint special "thanksgivings" therefor, and the blinded people shout and sing glory to God!!! "Crime" in high places eclipses it everywhere else. The functionaries in Church and State might be exchanged for the State prisoners with social advantage, were it not that the little scoundrels would so quickly become big ones, if they were put into the big scoundrel's situations; so outrageously and inevitably corrupting were those situations. And this is a fair sample of all the government the world had till the Good Time came.

War, pauper houses, gambling hells, false and fraudulent "churches," and all but spurious schools, bankrupt the entire "civilized" world. Half the women common harlots. The other half, (a few frightful old maids excepted) "married" to husbands who made, and generally contrive to keep those harlots. Naked mobs break into the banks, and ravage the palaces of shin-plaster barons and merchant princes, having previously demolished all the prisons. Culmination of the great religious, moral, and political hellishness. A cute Yankee cannonier and a French chemist put their wits and ingenuity together, and hatch up a plan whereby opposing armies can poison, or rather smother each other to death at eight or ten miles distance, in from five to thirty minutes, according to numbers. The annihilator can be dropped from a balloon, with effects equally fatal. Any city in the world can be reduced to a tomb in half an hour!! All the fortifications and battle ships utterly powerless against this invention. The whole human race—ay, all animated existence, at the mercy of this most infernal contrivance.

"Now," says Art, " I'm master of the situation, and I'll be the tool of folly and humbug no longer. You must send mysticism, moralism, and their attendant barbarities and fooleries to the bygones. You must have *me* for either your saviour or your destroyer; and I'll not wait long for your choice."

Panic of Government bond-holders and capitalists generally. Five hundred dollars in U. S. currency offered for one dollar in gold. British Government Stock goes begging at 1-2 penny a pound.— All other government stocks equally worthless.— Kings throw away their crowns, after selling the gold and jewels therein, and abandon their thrones, as terrified rats desert a house on fire. Universal panic and dismay. It is evident to all, that religious, moral, and political *constraint and violence* must stop at this point, or the human race be annihilated. Not the slightest faith in prayer and fasting can now for one moment be got up. The demagogues acknowledge that caucus and ballot-boxism is the wildest of Utopias and the most atrocious of swindles, and that it is clean played out. The everlasting discussionists admit the utter fallaciousness of their precious maxim, that "error may be safely trusted where *reason* is left free to combat it." The parsons, politicians, moralists, and let-aloneites tremblingly acknowledge that their quackeries are the sum of all quackeries. All the functionaries, both in Church and State, resign, and implore the scientists and artists to take their places. All their subjects eagerly back up the petition; even the mob stop their depredations and join in the new movement. The scientists and artists come to the rescue. They unite Church and State, *one and indivisible*, on a scientific basis—they organize THE UNIVERSAL MUTUAL GUARANTEE CO., which thenceforth, and forever, includes *all mankind*.

ACT XII.

INAUGURATION OF THE GOOD TIME.

Instant necessities of the people provided for.—A wise financier has rendered repudiation impossible in the largest nation, though the currency had there augmented till it was worth, *according to the old way of reckoning value*, little more than its weight in paper rags. The whole now funded in the *World's Government Stocks*—in shares of the UNIVERSAL MUTUAL GUARANTEE CO.; secured, not by prisons, gibbets, swords, bayonets, cannon, and gunpowder, wherewith to oppose and circumvent the Almighty, but by co-operative organization of labor, capital, and skill, for producing the means of fulfilling *the constitution and laws framed by the maker of human nature—for satisfying, instead of trying to repress human desire.* To that "Utopia" mankind come at last. Like magic, there arises in the "Great West," and all the other semi-deserts, palatial residences for the people, that rival the faith-built "mansions in the skies," with manufactories and agriculture to match. Savages and barbarians no longer stand contemptuously aloof; they embrace the new and *true* civilization with a perfect rush.— All the world embrace it with the utmost alacrity. Good by to barbarian metal currency. Farewell to that worse than barbarian institution, with unsurpassable impudence or stone-blindness, called "free-trade." Mutual and inexpensive, and undamaging interchange of products. The currency *directly* represents useful production. Capital perfectly assured, and all but infinitely more valuable than ever before. Invention goes ahead like magic. Science and art rapidly achieve greater perfection than even miracle-believers ever dared to hope for. Love fully emancipated. Women disenthralled. *Universal reciprocation of love, and Indissoluble Marriage of the whole Human Race, Present and Prospective.* Children begotten and provided for so that they become perfect men and perfect women, their *true* parent, the State, paying the expense, and reaping incalculable benefit thereby, even in a monied point of view. The car of progress speeds on to its goal. Tempests and volcanoes give way. The ice dissolves at both the poles, and luminosity becomes everywhere sufficient. All human desire is satisfied, with just the exertion requisite to give due pleasantness. Sickness is no more. Death is stripped of its terrors. People live till all conceivable delight palls on the five senses from repetition, and then resign their consciousness finally, with as little regret and fear as they go to sleep nightly. All mankind form a harmonious Social Organism. They are so situated that they can no more avoid doing right, than, under the old rickety rackety social contrivance, they could avoid doing wrong. CREATION IS FINISHED.

ACT XIII.

Glorious Panorama of Heaven on Earth. Exquisite Tableaux Vivants of *real Gods and Goddesses*. Complete and perfect reconciliation of Humanity with Divinity; they prove to be *immutably one, identical, and indivisible*. Celestial music. The world's Grand Anthem——" ALMIGHTY, THY WILL IS DONE."

END.

APPENDIX.

Two great Saturnalias of profligacy stand recorded ; and from present indications, a third will be added to the list; all within less than three centuries.

One of these Saturnalias grew out of the long, Dark Age of monkish austerity, and took place in France, the other, which Count Grammont's *Secret History of the Court of Charles the Second* so vividly and truly describes, was the fruit of the double and twisted austerity which Puritanism inflicted in England. A third, that will eclipse both the former, will soon come off in the United States, just so sure as the opposition to human nature which now so audaciously rears its Puritanical head goes on unchecked. The longer and stronger you oppose nature, the more violent and disastrous will be the reaction.

Two great laws are absolute; they can by no possibility be overcome. These are, gravitation, and the natural, "*God*"-given passions. To overcome the first, has never been seriously attempted ; but to circumvent the second—to invent " statutes" for crushing human nature out of men and women— has been almost the sole aim of government.

Superstition has hitherto been the most terrible

engine of persecution; but science having nearly spoiled that, another, (if it can fairly be called another) far more terrible, is fast coming into use; that other is—"*morality;*" how *much* more terrible this may possibly become, can easily be seen from the fact that *superstition* chiefly requires us to *believe*, or *pretend* to believe, contrary to our senses; whilst "*morality*" requires us to *really act* contrary to our senses—contrary to our most vehement natural feelings! Contrary to "God Almighty"—put whatever construction you can on that name. Superstition and "morality" are complements of each other, and always went hand in hand; still, the main object of persecution has been to enforce the former; considerable indulgence was openly given to the latter, by the Papists; and it is in evidence that even the Puritans granted indulgencies *sub rosa*, to all whom they could not otherwise rope into their policy. Walter Scott charges that they chiefly rebuked the King—Charles The First—for being so open in his gallantries.

But the great object of both the Papist and Puritan leaders now is *money;* if they can get plenty of that, they don't care a fig what you or I or anybody believes or disbelieves. And in order to get plenty of money, they must preach "morality;" *miracle* having become the laughing stock of the age.

"Morality" is the sub basis of persecution: (I have demonstrated that it is, in the last analysis, pure superstitition and impossibleness)—its fundamental axiom is to treat others as well as you treat yourself, with no proposition for treating yourself to anything better than *constraint and* "*self-denial!*"

[Self-denial? Poh! Talk about lifting yourself by your waistbands; and done with it.]

But I have discovered how we can treat ourselves and *everybody else* infinitely better than we ever before have done; I have found out the law of human nature's full and complete satisfaction as the attentive reader of my book thus far knows.

Church and State can, as I have shown, actualize "Heaven" on Earth; but they will be only a stupendous nuisance, such as they always have been, till they organize labor, capital, skill, and love affairs, *so that every man and every woman can act just as they naturally please to act.*

In the "Dark Ages," the wonderful results of machinery had scarcely begun to be manifest. Railroads were not built. Electro-dynamics were comparatively unknown. And Mutual Insurance, and Joint Stock Corporations, and that great preliminary link of the Social Organism—national paper currency—were not carried to an extent that could give even a glimmering preconception of their all-important significancy. And in the palmiest days of Greece and Rome, there was still more plausibility in the cruel and senseless Procrusteanism of forcing people to "subdue their passions," and be "content with little." Now, the case is widely different. If there *can be* such a thing as criminal foolishness, you, ye moralists, are guilty of it.

You have the effrontery to tell us we must not "do evil that good may come." Must we not, though? Must we not, *so long as you have rule*, ever and anon slaughter millions on millions of human beings, that government may be kept up?—in the hopes that good may somehow come out of that government? *Must* we not, "in time of peace"—if mere armistice can be called peace—"prepare for war?" And *you* tell us we must not do evil that good may come; *you* with a long, hypocritical face, that the "Devil" himself must despise unless you have taught him new devilishness; you tell us this, too, when it is proposed to raise by raffling, or wine-selling at a fair, the means wherewith to *partly* assuage the unutterable woes your moral foolery and worse than infernal vindictiveness have inflicted! Why, you precious numskulls, don't you know that your Lord Jehovah once set up the holy apostleship at a raffle? If you don't believe it just turn to Acts I., 26. And did it never occur to you how extravagantly your blessed "saviour" passed round the wine, even to people who had "well drunk," at the wedding in "Cana of Galilee?"

Moral Principleites! If it had been your *special aim* to destroy the happiness of mankind, and multiply misery, rascality, corruption, and all that is vile, how *could* you have done all this more effectually than you have? I defy you to describe a worse *possible* state of things than always has taken place under your administration.

"But," methinks I hear some "moral" sniveller exclaim; "if it hadn't been for the infidels, and the gamblers, and the rum-sellers, and the theatres, and the "———

Pheugh! What is your "moral" nostrum good for if, in the course of countless ages, with a *vast majority* of the world's wealth, and respectability, and influence, to back up and recommend it, it has *worse and worse failed* to counteract all that has been, or could have been, opposed to the well-being of mankind?

What would you say to doctors who should persist in using medicines, under the operation of which their patients grew worse and worse? Would you not call them the most impudent of charlatans, if they should tell you that their medicine was perfectly good, and that it would certainly cure only for this symptom or that symptom of the disease?

And what would you call such quacks if they should try their meanest to prevent any and everyone from saying, writing, or printing anything against their quackery—anything calculated to open the eyes of the public in regard to it? I'll tell you what I should call them. I should call them just such diabolical scoundrels as nine in ten of you are, who are not fools. You stick at no means, however despicable, whereby to suppress everything calculated to expose and upset your ignorance-enveloped, or most deeply hidden, and most treacherously and dangerously masked hellishness.

And you cant against "blasphemy," and lying; yet in the same breath you utter that most atrocious blasphemy — that damnedest of lies—"necessary evil."

"But haven't the clergy, the moralists, and the politicians, done a great deal of good, after all? Look at the superior civilization of Europe and America," again snivels the sniveller.

Don't be deceived by that magnificent and most vaguely-general term, "civilization." Deduct from civilization all the good that material art has done, and there will remain only the mystical and moral barbarism which Europe stole from Asia, where it was learned in schools as savage as any that ignorance now keeps in the most heathenish part of Africa. That mystical and moral savagery, our Puritan forefathers cursed America with. Every moral saying found in the New Testament, which statesmen quote, and infidels so stupidly admire, is found, *verbatim*, in the writings of those speculative old heathens—Confucius and Plato—who lived many centuries before A.D., and they stole the very pith of it from the savage ignorance that didn't know how to satisfy, and therefore undertook to repress human nature.

"We take it for granted," says a most respectable New York daily paper of March 22, of the eighteen hundred and sixty-fourth "*year of our Lord*," "that the statements made at a meeting of workingwomen held last night are in the main correct. These statements, which appear in another column, we have not time just now, to discuss at length; but let us ask a question: If you, reader had a sister who was compelled to try to support life on making men's fine shirts at *sixteen cents each*, and find her own thread, where would you look for that sister in twelve months? Assuming these statements to be true, it is inexpressibly infamous that such a state of things should exist in a city pretending to be civilized."

Moralism and Christianism done any good? *Pah!* They stink to the very heavens. But I'll tell you 'where that sister would be found in less than *three* months, if she persisted in being " virtuous" (?) (Is suicide virtuous? and which is most virtuous; slow or instant suicide?) and had no dependance but her needle. Listen :—

A while ago I was poorer than I now am—so poor that I lived in a house, in a street quite opposite, as to quality, to the Fifth Avenue, and in the story next the garret. Certain fragile forms used to flit past me up or down stairs, in a manner indicating a desire to avoid observation. One dreadful night in December, I was aroused from sleep by the most heartrending cries. I sprang from my bed, threw a blanket over me, and rushed to the hall. There stood shivering two of the forms aforesaid, if they could fairly be called more than shadows. "Oh, Mr.! do come up ; she's dead! she's dead!" I followed them up a ladder into the garret, where I could stand erect only under the ridgepole. In this rough boarded hole stood a sugar loaf sized and shaped stove, with a tailor's goose on top, and a pan of coal siftings alongside. On a rough packing-box that answered for a table, a dirty newspaper was spread for a cloth.— Two cracked plates, two rusty knives and forks, a tin tea-pot, two broken backed wooden chairs, and a stool comprised the rest of the apartment's furnishing, except a straw bed on the bare floor, with cast off female garments for its scanty covering. On this bed lay the sister of the the two weeping skeletons who had aroused me. There she lay, starved, benumbed, suffocated, and worked to death!

In less than three weeks, the same woful scene was enacted over again! Another of the sisters, not more than seventeen years of age, an American girl, and one whom nature formed prettier than the average, had been tortured to death at making gentlemen's (?) vests at prices utterly inadequate to "keep body and soul together." The only remaining sister left this " religious" and moral hell, and I never found out what became of her. But I do know that a Legislature well schooled in Christianism and moralism, and fully aware that thousands of such Hells as I have just described exist within their political sphere, cover up their ignorance as to the remedy by passing laws to punish hugging and kissing in lager bier saloons, and prevent the working people from healthful recreation on Sunday!

At the workingwomen's meeting above mentioned, a *soi pensant* benevolent individual of the genus *moral*, roared out most vindictively for the names of the employers who paid the poor women such starvation wages. Look ye, old foo-foo, the first time you consult your looking-glass, you'll see *one* of those mean, contemptible employers stareing you plumply in the face. Don't you buy your vests and pants, and shirts as cheap as you can? and isn't the partaker of stolen life, time, money, or other property, as bad as the thief, and a devilish sight meaner? Away with the mawkish sensibility and innocent foolishness, that relishes a nice bit of lamb, but hates and despises the "cruel butcher."

The social mountebanks by whose quackish experiments mankind have been tortured ever since "the beginning," tell us we have evil desires which must be repressed. What blasphemous nonsense! Who gave us those desires? I say there are *no* evil desires. Thieves, murderers, *politicians even*, do but desire happiness. All the evil in the case is owing to ignorance as to method. The only practical method is the religious, or universal application of physical science and art. *Ars artium Hominorum Salvator est.*

For countless ages, the quacks who dabble in mystery, morality, and utterly vexatious and uncertain law, have been trying, alternately through brutal kings and swindling demagogues, to repress nature, and *thus* make people better. And fraud, corruption, cruelty, and injustice are all but triumphant! And prostitution, that ineradicable damnation spot on "moral" civilization, has attained proportions greater than ever before! And war and its more and more horrible paraphrenalia are fast rendering every nation in the world bankrupt! And the people of a single Christian nation, and that nation the most favored of all, have butchered each other to the extent of at least 2,000,000 of their most able bodied men, and damaged themselves and other nations to the amount of more than $10,000,000,000 in less than four years!

And Christian and Moral Europe has just commenced (Feb. 20, "1864") the largest harvest of the infernal part of religio-moralism, that even she has ever yet rept. The bloodiest wars the world ever experienced will, from all appearances, take place between the 1864th and 1874th "*year of our Lord.*" And you preach *this* "sublimely moral" religion of "*peace on earth and good will to men,*" with as much effrontery as you could if it had been a perfect success, instead of the most woful and shameful failure that can possibly take place!

And the "Lobby," with corruption funds *ad libitum*, is notoriously the controlling legislative body! And the police and magistracy are in alliance with the most atrocious scoundrels! They extort immense sums of money from common prostitutes, and often go shares with pickpockets, forgers, and burglars! And a vast amount of money which goes to sustain the highly "moral Christian Church," comes from the rent of brothels, the winnings of gambling hells, the profits on strychnined liquors, and those wholesale murder concerns, swill milk stables. Much of it is extorted from harlots, or black-mailed from their keepers and overseers by threats of arrest! But the filthiest lucre of all, is that so lavishly bestowed on that highly "moral" "Church" by those meanest of thieves, who have defrauded it from their creditors, and by those highly respectable *modern* saints, who daily perpetrate the most atrocious swindles at the stock exchange. No where else except in "Church," should we so earnestly pray, "deliver us from evil." And we must not do evil that good may come? eh? Catch a parson refusing $5,00 that a harlot had just earned at her trade! or $500 that a legislator had just received for perjuriously selling his vote to carry the enactment of some most atrocious law! Catch a parson refusing such filthy lucre as this; I'd just like to see him; and Barnum would make twice as much by exhibiting him, as he did by showing us the "What Is It?"

And every town has its pauper-house, every

county its jail, every state its prison, all crammed full of human woe! And the streets swarm with beggars, and none of us are a single moment safe from counterfeiters, thieves, pickpockets, burglars, highwaymen and murders!

Mysteryites, moralists, and politicians! These are your fruits! Have you the brassfacedness to deny it? Well, then, you can't be so fool-hardy as to say they are not your failures! And is not that just as bad? ay, worsé, so long as you persist in those failures!

Infidels! A word in your ear; for *you* are the stupidest moralists that I know of. Turn to your dictionary; what do you see? "*Immorality.*—any act or practice which contravenes the *divine commands* or the social duties." A very comprehensive word, is immorality, you see. A most effectively masked double-barrelled battery, shooting both ways, will the "moral principle" artillery prove, if it can only get provided with plenty of brute force to man it, and legal ammunition to charge it with.

Parsons, Politicians, and Moralists! Your whole system is the best possible contrivance for encouraging and perpetuating magnificent crime, for discountenancing, persecuting, injuring, and *disgracing* all who don't succeed in villainy, and for covering honesty with contempt. Is anything more pitiable, (alias contemptible) than poverty? Do you seek, or *avoid* proximity to the meanly clad, hard fisted laborer, while in *any* public place? And do you feel disgraced by shaking hands with those army contractors—those incarnate fiends, who have made princely fortunes by exposing our country's brave defenders to perish of cold and wet in shoddy blankets, and by poisoning them to death with putrid meat? Do not you feel complimented when they offer you a velvet cushioned seat beside them in church during the sacrament?

I would bet my "soul's" salvation, if I had a "soul," that had the "war in Heaven" given victory to its instigator, the "Devil" would now be your adored "God," and "God" would be your abhored "Devil;" nor would your "religion," your "law," your "moral principle," need the slightest alteration, except an interchange of names, in order to fit the case.

Mysteryites, Moralists, Politicians, and Skeptics! I command you to turn right about and embrace the *Gospel of Science*, and the *Politics of Art*. Disobey, and I condemn you to full participation in the torments your fooleries inflict. You'll not find this a bull against the comet, and may "God," if there is a "God," have mercy on your "souls," if you've got any "souls."

Parsons, Politicians, Moralists, and Skeptics! When, from all eternity, did you ever cobble up a government wherein it was not perfectly sure that sooner or later civil war would *actualize* "Hell on Earth?"

And when you get our Demagoguery cobbled up again, do you even profess to hope that it will last longer than what you call "a great while?" I will bet a gold dollar against a worn out postage stamp, that it will not, on *your* plan, last so long as did the one that has just squummux'd into military rule

North, and perfect "Hell" South, and that it will be a still *faster* rampage of corruption and devilishness even at that. *Not but that I go for the Union against Secesh, on* ANY *terms*—Secesh being out of the pale of hope, which Union, however demagogueish, is not. Even you, ye cursed demagogues, can't wean *me* from the Union. For *I* know that Union will, in spite of you and your associate fiends, be a *real liberty Union*, that will include the whole world. If I did not know this—if I firmly believed, as *almost* every body does, in an everlasting round of "self denial," monarchy, war, and demagoguery—in the perpetuation of a social contrivance that degrades all labor to performance by whip dreading Negroes or starvation impelled white slaves, I would say,—let secession, even to its last analysis, come now; the sooner the better. Why not? Is it not generally admitted, ay, evident, that, as things are,

"The world is all a fleeting show;
For man's illusion given?"

Is it not still a question among philosophers, whether the rich are not as much to be pitied in their gilded misery, as the poor are in their squalid wretchedness? Is not suicide *more* common among the former than among the latter?

The barriers thrown in Nature's way by moralists, stimulate her to such abnormal strength and activity, that she *much more* than overcomes them. All historians agree, that when marriage was abolished in

France,* prostitution very sensibly diminished. Shut a dog up in a room where, if the door was open, he would be content to remain all day, and he will try to get out as soon as he discovers that he is confined. Tell a child he *must* do the very thing he wants to; and unless he is a very dull and stupid child he will hesitate. But moralists can't see anything but their own narrow, gloomy, bigoted speculations, and what's the use of talking to such dolts? I am addressing *some*, at least, who can see things other than through the spectacles of old Granny Habit.

"What would become of the children, if marriage was abolished?" In "God Almighty's" name, what becomes of them now? Let prisons, gibbets, pauper-houses, prostitution dens, and *war* answer. If society did not make it disgraceful for *natural* parents to provide for their offspring, they would do so, even now. It is a proverb, that "it is better to be a lord's bastard than his younger son." Why? Because a lord is above careing for what society thinks in this case, and therefore provides better for his bastards than he does for his younger sons.

What do you say to passing a law authorizing every man and every woman to *suit themselves in their love affairs*, and appropriating a sufficient sum to thoroughly educate all children, grammatically,

---

* Napoleon and Josephine lived many loving years together without being married. Their "wedding" did not take place till the day before their coronation; and that wedding was, in all probability, the main cause of their separation. See Thiers' "Consulate and Empire."

arithmetically, geographically, and *physically*, and *provide* for them, so that they will *all* have *useful*, attractive, and sufficiently remunerative employment?

"That would be against the Constitution?" the Constitution be damned. I tell you that until we have *just* that law, and *exactly* that appropriation, we shall, at shorter and shorter intervals, have a *conscription law*, an *appropriation for butchering men and starving women and children by millions*, and an intermediateness of lobbyism, mercenary prostitution, pauperism, cruelty, and as perfect injustice and damnation as *physical science and art* will permit.

Do, I beseech you, let me be fairly understood, on this all-important subject. I say, let society place all its members so that, in order to get a living, the men will not be compelled to cheat and murder each other, nor will the women be constrained to prostitute themselves for life or by the job. Situate all men and women so that they can freely act out their nature. If nature—"God's" law, *believers* can't deny—prompts us to restrict our love to one, *so be it*. If *nature* prompts us to bestow our love ever so promiscuously, *why not thus bestow it?* If some people *naturally* want to bind themselves, let them do so, ever so tightly; but why, in the name of all that is not stark, starving madness or most infernal tyranny, shall such be permitted to fasten their fetters on others?

I tell you that the *perfect* freedom I have pictured in this book, is sure to come, sooner or later; that mystical and moral hellishness will, *comparatively* soon, crush under their own weight, a perfect Nemesis, and mankind will go to "Heaven" via "Hell," unless they take a shorter cut. The best will come, *in spite of the worst*, not by means of it, as our "all for the best" Dr. Panglosses tell us. Perfection is the goal to which *substantial* existence irrepressibly tends. The "irrepressible conflict" is between nature on the one side, and all the short sighted scoundrels and stone blind fools on the other; and I'll stake my reputation on the complete success of nature, and *thorough and everlasting emancipation of mankind and womankind from all constraint whatever.*

Nor will this take place by slow degrees. Mankind follow leaders as naturally and inevitably as planets revolve around the sun; and they will follow their leaders from "Hell" to "Heaven," just as a flock of sheep jump over the fence after the bell weather, from a bad pasture to a good one. And the leaders will jump this fence just as soon as they learn the "*Religion of Science*," and the simple fact that by no other means can they secure *their own happiness.*

ADDENDA.

ORIGIN, AND CRITICAL ANALYSIS OF "MORAL PRINCIPLE."

WHEN, in the course of material development, mankind were created, experience was null, and understanding at zero. As fancy had not anything to check its flight, it manufactured the Universe out of nothing, decreed almightiness to *will*, (consider this; thoroughly) and promised the "Heaven"-instinct which distinguishes mankind from lower animals, *full satisfaction after death!* full swing in those blissful realms of free love, where they " neither marry nor are given in marriage ;" an everlasting " blow out," where they have no need to " be content with little ;" the everyday apparel being "white robes" of a celestial fineness, the dwellings being too magnificent for minute description, the common highways "streets of gold." All which, involves the transcendancy of mind, spirit, will, or fancy over matter, invests mere function with independency of, and arbitrary control over *organ!* The assumption in the case is, that will is a *cause*—that it can direct physical action ; but the fact is, that will is a mere function—a mere *effect* dependent on natural, physical, cerebal organization, *subjectively*, and on external materiality or its consequents, *objectively*. And this falsely and ignorantly supposed transcendency of mind, will, or " spirit," is the sole justification for that vindictiveness which has added wrong to wrong, till the abominable heap has, in "Secession," reached dimensions that cannot possibly be exceeded.

"Moral principle" mongers ! Behold the fruit of countless ages of your fooleries ! Christians ! Behold the result of almost nineteen centuries' trial of your " moral" Gospel's " peace on earth !" The people more favoured by *national position* [mind this] and, *in spite of you*, by *science and art*, [always keep this prominently in view] than any other, are, nevertheless, stuck so brim full of the "gospel" and "moral principle" which prevent science and art from forming a religio-governmental basis, [here's a study for those who would be *true* liberators] that they are, in the very infancy of their nationality, exhausting their wealth and energies, and taxing, to the ruination point, the wealth and energies of many unborn generations, *in butchering each other !*

I tell you, ye "moral principle" mongers, that with the world's wealth and influence to back you from "the beginning," you are more "criminal" for failing to prevent all this evil, than you would be, had you *directly*, and *professedly*, caused it. For you have persistently encumbered the path of progress. You have blocked up the entrance to the *real* " kingdom of Heaven," with your science insulting, liberty mocking abstractions. You have usurpingly prevented the *enthronement* of that only true—that only possible " saviour"—*Material Art.*

The "Holy Scriptures" tell us that "The Devil can transform himself into an angel of light."— Strange that I, who don't attach "holiness" to *any* scriptures, should be the first to search for and find the "Prince of Devils" metamorphosed into that brightest and most angelic of appearances—"moral principle!"

The cruelest monsters that ever disgraced the human form were such from " moral principal." The Inquisition, and all the religious persecution that ever took place, had "moral principle" for their *deepest root.* "Morality!" "Virtue!" "Disinterestedness!" loudest howled Robespierre, Marat, and Fouquier Tinville.

All the variously named, though scarcely different natured governments are founded on "moral principle;" on the monstrous assumption that *instinct* should be but very limitedly indulged! that people ought to sacrifice self! that *all* should relinquish *natural* rights—should largely forego the gratification of *natural desires*, individually, for the benefit of *all, collectively!* States thus become agglomerations of miniature treasons, as sure to breed insurrections and rebellions, as gunpowder would be sure to explode by friction, if every kernel was locomotive and irritable.

"Be to thine own self true, thou canst not then be false to any man," is but half of a most important fact, the counterpart to which is—" Be to thine ownself *false*, thou canst not then be true to any man." Yet "moral principle" requires people to "subdue their passions," "be content with little," almost wholly repress their most vehement *natural desires*, and, in short, be as *false to themselves* as they possibly can be, without committing *instant* suicide! So false, cruel, and unnatural, that the *mockery* that passes for life, does not average one-eighth the possible length of *real* life.

You can just as possibly lift yourself by your waistbands, as you can " subdue your passions "Try both experiments, and see if you can determine, after *thorough* examination, which has furnished most evidence that you are a fool. If mankind were "content with little," how could, or why should progress have made a single step?

But "moral principle," even as "divinely" taught, does not require people to love others *better* than they love themselves, and they therefore "enact" laws, and resort to violence, to *enforce on others, the cruelty they treat themselves to.* Hence wrong, oppression. and evil are perpetual, and treason periodical. Hence one great cause why the government of *compound* sovereigns—majorities—is always more oppressive, and far sooner productive of national ruin, than is the government of *richer*, and more luxurious *single* sovereigns. Hence there never has existed a state, wherein it was more than a mere question of time when there would be that horror of horrors—civil war, *Can* people, in the main, be more true, more just, more merciful to others than to their own selves? Does not every individual injury damage the whole community, whether such injury be self-inflicted or otherwise?

ATHEISM.

The only dangerous atheist is the church. She proclaims that God is an immaterial spirit, and thus practically denies his existence, while treacherously seeming to affirm it. God is all that *materially*, however *etherially*, exists. There cannot possibly be any other God.

ANARCHY.

While States, as now constituted, seemingly maintain some slight degree of order, they are generating *critical anarchy*. They periodicalize Saturnalias of anarchy. There never has been a government under which it was not perfectly sure, that, sooner or later, " civil war" would break out.

A DREAM.

I dreamed that the "war for the Union" was ended; that Jeff Davis, Beauregard, Floyd, and other infernals who headed Secession, had retired to Mexico, richly laden with spoils, and that all lesser rebels were pardoned, and restored to *friendly* and *honourable* citizenship. Whereupon the "criminals" confined in one of those " Hells" called a State Prison, tumultuously met in the yard, and "Resolved: —That we are the smallest villains and therefore the greatest fools in the world. Why did'nt we go it on a big figure ?"

"I," said a highwayman, " never killed more than half a dozen human bipeds. Faugh! Jeff. is the boy. He and his chaps knew how to secure wealth and *respect*. They murdered twenty or thirty thousand at a time! And they stole or destroyed more, during each week of their career, than such contemptible little rogues as we are have stolen or destroyed since the world began! Yet England, the most Christian, moral, and law-abiding government on earth, could scarcely restrain her impatience to clasp hands with Jeff. and his confederates, and welcome them among the rulers of mankind! And England's divinity students at famous Oxford, gave three cheers for Jeff.; cheers heartier than they ever before bestowed on a foreigner! And there's Alexander "The Great," and William "The Conqueror," and Pizarro, and Fernando Cortez. They murdered by millions, and robbed by thousands of millions. Yet grave historians, whose works all "*respectable libraries*" contain, laud them to the skies!"

"I," said a forger, "am here for passing a counterfeit two-dollar note on a bank, the worthlessness of every bill on which was discovered, just as I had produced one more of the same sort. The "President, Directors, and Company," of that and similar banking institutions in the "Great West," palmed off "bogus" to the amount of over nine million dollars in a few years. And some of *these* swindlers are judges, governors, and senators! *Them's um.*— Why hadn't *we* gumption enough to corrupt the legislatures to grant us "charters" to flood the whole country with "currency" as false as was that contemptible two dollar "shin plaster" that landed me here?"

A pale-faced wretch, whose "crime" consisted in robbing a hen-roost, to prevent his family from starving when they couldn't get shirts to make at six cents apiece, suggested that if society fairly understood the comparative nothingness of *punishable* "crime," pity would induce——

"Pity be damn'd!" roared all the others. "We want to be *honoured;* and *respected*; and we at length see clearly how; *don't* we though?"

Just then, the mutinous "rascals" heard the guard coming to shoot them down, and they scampered to their cells fully resolved to become "great" and "glorious" if they ever got a chance.

Parsons, Politicians, and morality mongers! Did any of you ever dream such a dream as this?

Devotees of "moral principle!" Do not you worse *despise* the thief than the assassin? the assassin than the brigand or pirate? the brigand or pirate than the soldierly secessionist? And would not *you* rather be feared—abhorred, even, than despised? And if Secession should triumph, will it not be "His Excellency," Jefferson Davis? and "The Honourable" Messrs. Floyd, Toombs, and so on, down to the "Esqrs.," around whose rebellious necks you would now, if *you could*, twist the death halter? And will not the highest toned in "moral principle" among you be as ready to trade with the thieves and murderers of Secessia, should she *be successful*, as with the New Englanders, provided you can make as large profits? Will you not, when the war is over, invite to your family alliance, even, Secessionists whose wealth you know was procured in serving the rebellion? whilst you spurn from your presence the petty larceny convict who has served out his sentence? And why do you despise him, if not because his villainy is *too small* for your admiration—too diminutive for your tolerance, even?

You "don't despise those who are not criminals, either large or small?" Show me such. I tell you that all mankind compose one vast sinner, and that you are now reading the repentance wail of an awakened part of that sinner.

You "don't cheat, nor rob, nor murder?" Then you wear no shirt, no pants, no coat, no boots or shoes; nay, you eat no food: nay, you don't even read a newspaper; for these are all produced at a great sacrifice of human life, as you well know, if you are not criminally negligent. You can neither buy nor sell, without conniving with a cheat system, whereby labor is degraded to performance by whip-dreading Negroes, or starvation impelled white slaves.

I tell you, that what passes for government is an inheritance from barbarism. It is, and ever has been, the world over, a system of wholesale bigandage; a system of cruelty and injustice that cannot be surpassed.

FABLE.

A convicted swindler being asked by the judge what he had to say before being sentenced, replied: "My guilt is nothing compared to that which you help to uphold. I only obtained five dollars by a false pretence; your so-called 'religion' has obtained the world's wealth many times over; yet it is a pretence so abominably false as not to admit of the least particle of even the questionable evidence which your sham law allows. Its priests, coolly and unblushingly say that it is a '*mystery!*'" And all the so-called 'governments' pretend to make life secure, yet they kill people every hour in the day in the most secure times, and periodically, and at very short intervals, slaughter mankind by wholesale. As to their pretence to make property secure, why, judge, they destroy as far as the *art-element in civilization* will let them, *all* security. What you call 'the Word of God' declares that under these governments 'riches take to themselves wings and fly away.' But I am also charged with assaulting the officer who arrested me. Well, don't *all* governments (and *all* religions sanction them) educate their people to consider fighting the most glorious of all professions or occupations? Now, judge, I am ready for the finishing stroke of that monster injustice, one of whose ministers you are. All I ask is, that you will not interlard my sentence with any of the hypocritical cant and electioneering gammon, usual on such occasions."

"His Honor" gave the "rascal" seven years; two for the swindle and assault, and five for contempt of court.

Moral. — In order to swindle successfully, go about it in a pious and "lawful" way; and if a Tiger gets his paws on you, don't touch his sore spot.

MESSRS. LEGISLATORS! LISTEN!

The magistrates for the county of Berks, in England, communicated to the London Times of December 10, in the eighteen-hundred-and-sixtieth year of "our blessed Lord and Saviour," (?) a statement respecting the condition of the peasantry in nineteen towns and villages, as "a fair sample of the condition of the agricultural laboring population of England." "Our peasantry," remarks the Times, on this communication, " are far worse lodged than our beasts of burden. Parents and adult children, and brothers and sisters, men and women grown, crowdedly sleep in the same room, and often in the same bed together, *pell-mell*, and some daughters have as many as four bastards!" Bastards begot through the vilest incest!!

And this is Christian and moral England! The very bulwark of "holy matrimony!" And England's rulers cant so edifyingly against French licentiousness! And England is more afraid than any nation on earth, except Puritanical Scotland, (that has more drunkards and bastards in proportion to her inhabititants, than has any other nation) that if marital bondage is abolished, or even loosened, promiscuous intercourse and licentiousness will result!— And England's rulers, in apparent ignorance of the above-described state of things, spend their time over a law to decide whether a man may or may not marry his deceased wife's sister!!!

And our own Legislators, who compose part of a government so unscientifically botched up that more than a million of its people have died in their bloom by each other's hands within little more than three years, fritter away their time over Sunday Laws and Concert Saloon Bills!!

The social quacks of old, did "strain at a gnat and swallow a camel." Modern social quacks may as fairly be said to strain at the smallest gnat's egg, and swallow the largest comet, tail and all.

STANDING ARMIES AND NAVIES.

Oh, my country, beware of chronic war!—of *standing* armies and navies! All the material of field warfare, and the four hundred battle-ships that we have built, let us sell to other nations as soon as secession is put down, and then inaugurate a *real liberty polity* that will "sweetly force" those nations to convert their horrible purchase, together with their own Hell-machinery, to rail-road iron, farming utensils, and oven wood. That would be a ,'Yankee trick" that would place the extra " smartness" of "Young America" beyond question. And what a financial system it would give rise to. The state stocks of the nations—the debt that had been plunged into for oppressing mankind and trying to subvert nature —would form the basis of a currency for perfectly liberating human nature, and harmoniously adjusting the Social Organism that all mankind compose, with the Universal Organism, or all that is humanly cognizable. There is no other possible way, whereby the "Hell"-debt of the world can be liquidated; and in this way the United States alone could pay it in two generations.

ORGANIZATION OF LOVE ON THE FREE PRINCIPLE.

Able bodied and able headed producers make all the wealth the world has, or can have. Then, in the name of all that is not stark stareing madness or slavering idiosy, "let population thrive" by the means best calculated to make it the best possible. Let children come and welcome as fast as *love* can produce them. Are not those children in utter disregard to natural, *real* legitimacy called "bastards" proverbially smarter than those begotten in hate inspiring monogamy, notwithstanding society throws all the disadvantages in their way that she possibly can?

If love was unchained, *all* natural mothers honoured, and *all natural* offspring cared for as most precious acquisitions to the State; if half the expense of the present horrible Saturnalia of political unwisdom had been expended in remodelling society in accordance with free love, (of course, I would not encroach on the right of any who chose bondage in love) population, wealth, magnificence, and *practical* right would increase so rapidly—-Nature would accomplish her grand aim so suddenly, that were I to attempt description, it would be looked upon as a new chapter in the "Arabian Nights." It would seem as impossible as the electro magnetic telegraph seemed twenty years ago; as fictitious as a description of New York, London, or Paris, would appear to savages, who had never heard of any practicabilities superior to their wretched huts, canoes, and hunting implements.

Three or four generations such as free love and its social requisites would produce, would eliminate "the iniquities of the fathers,"—the innumerable diseases which stagnating monogamy *chiefly* produces and entails—and forever purge man of evil. If the cash cost of the present rebellion had been invested in unobstructing the production, and aiding the rearing of *natural* children, as scientifically as money is invested in the cultivation of Lorton blackberries, even, the profits of that investment, in a purely financial point of view, would, in one generation, be too great to be calculated in dollars.

If all the prostitution entailing, adultery perpetuating, infanticide compelling, wife and husband murder inciting, love extinguishing laws that "play hell" with the sexual, social, political, and all other human relations, were abrogated, premiums offered by the State for the stoutest and handsomest babies, and honours decreed to their *natural* mothers, oh, "Heaven," what a change would come. "In a moment, in the twinkling of an eye," in comparison to former progress, splendid and joyous palaces, such as faith mistakenly builds in the regions of nowhere, would displace the isolated abodes of jealousy, dreariness, idiosy, insanity, venerea, prolapsus uteri, consumption, hysteria, hypochondria, superstition, and "moral principle." In these palaces love would be universally reciprocal. Men and women, as beautiful and everyway as perfect in body as they hope to be in "spirit," would luxuriate in each other's embraces, changing partners as often as nature, under the healthiest possible treatment by art, prompted. Fairy like music, the fragrance of sweetest flowers, and the most elegant surroundings imaginable would lend their charms to the conception delights, that would send forth beings to live—*really* live, hundreds of years; ay, till sensation became satisfied with every possible variety of pleasurableness.

The sole business of government should be, not to repress, *but satisfy all human desire.* For mankind have *no* evil desires; they do but desire happiness; all the evil in the case arises from ignorance as to method. Kings, demagogues, secessionists, and *common* robbers, swindlers, and murderers do but pursue happiness, oh! how ignorantly. Think, capitalists, how incalculably more delightful and safe it would be to pocket the interest paying "green backs" and know that they represented the amount of evil abolished,—that they were invested in, and secured by a free, joyous, wealth amassing population, instead of paying for devastation and human butchery—instead of paying to kill off traitors [and getting killed by them] so that they would not need killing off again for "a great while"—for fifty years perhaps; the most hopeful say one hundred; but I do not see how it can be twenty, if our rulers persist in trying to enforce that utter impossibleness, "moral principle."

A VISION.

It seemed as though I was among a people who, instead of studying how to make nature their friend and ally, were carrying on a war of subjugation against her; insanely imagining her to be "depraved," and hostile to their highest interests. Confusion of course had a continuous holiday; folly was rampant, and ignorance supreme.

Although in this country, food ready cooked grew spontaneously and in great abundance, I observed that the people were ravenously hungry; and that very many were actually dying of starvation, or languishing on beds of sickness in consequence thereof.

I was not long, however, in discovering that the cause of all this was the prevalence of a notion that spoiling the appetite in every possible way, and denying the stomach the food it naturally craved, was the most sublime and meritorious of virtues, and the surest and most approved mark of "practical piety"—a sort of subjective commodity of no determinate value, yet in the highest repute.

The instant I prepared to appease my own appetite, I was most unceremoniously apprized that, contrary to all appearances, nothing was more difficult —that there was a "law" written out in due form in their frightfully ponderous statute book, prohibiting people from taking *any* food, except by sucking it through a very narrow tube.

But I instantly perceived that the real basis of all this "piety," "virtue," and "law" was the fear that if people ate as much as they pleased, they would consequently grow so large, that both clothing and even shelter, would be inadequate; these being produced only in such niggardly quantities as the all but wholly isolated efforts of individuals could furnish them; the government devoting itself entirely to the business of being, by *some* means, and in *some* shape, no matter how or what, at the head of affairs; and never dreaming that it was its business to take measures for securing to the governed, abundance of clothing and shelter, and thus exemption from evil consequent on eating their fill; too much present delight, it was generally feared, might divert man's affection from the eternal revel in which he was instructed to expect to indulge *after death;* besides, for government to interfere with individuals, except by way of taxing, humbugging and punishing them, would be to distrust the people's capability to take care of themselves, each on his or her "own hook;" and would be such a gross infringement on the people's individual rights, and such a death-blow to "individual responsibility" or "virtue," that it was most strictly guarded against in their vaunted Palladium of liberty—"*The Constitution.*" The policy was, to compel every individual to clothe and house himself or herself and family, as he or she, with the least possible co-operation with others, best could; and of course to scrimp all in food, and thus curtail them in size, to that degree that they might, without public aid or private charity, and above all without reciprocal assistance.

and consequent damage to private "virtue,""morality" and "independence," be as well housed and clothed as they ought to expect to be in " the present evil world."

In some of the Provinces or States, the government furnished tubes at a price fixed by statute;— in other parts of the country they were sold by a class priveleged to demand the statute price for them; and in a very few places any one might give them away, upon certain conditions, provided that they were of the legal dimensions.

But this absurd law, instead of preventing natural eating, did but augment surreptitious gluttony to such a degree that what obtained the name of " the shameful disease" was, either virulently, or in some of its chronic forms, almost universal. It became even transmissible by contact; and there was scarcely a family, however punctilious, which was untainted.

Also, food taken through " the tube," as might rationally have been foreseen, irritated, stimulated, and unnaturally enlarged, instead of satisfying, the appetite. And as all eating *sans* tube, had, under severe penalties, to be done in secret, it was performed in such hot haste, in order to make the most of the opportunity, that many thus ravenously swallowed more food in a single day, than they would, if left to their own free choice, have eaten in a month; thus often making themselves so sick, however, that they actually diminished instead of increasing in size; which was considered both a public gain—a " necessary evil"—and a just punishment of those immediately concerned.

From the best information obtainable, it was a safe calculation that more than half the people dispensed with the use of the tube whenever they got a sly chance, despite the legal penalties, and notwithstanding the care with which they were educated to look on a violation of the tube law as the lowest disgrace. And it must be obvious, that in order to prevent the unscrupulous, especially when half-starved, from breaking such a law, a constable would be needed for every citizen, a deputy sheriff for every constable, a high sheriff for every deputy, and so on. The " conscience" was the main dependance, after all ; (although it became a standing proverb, that " an empty stomach had no conscience;') and no pains were spared by those short-sighted enough to imagine it for their interest to perpetuate this unnatural, absurd and hypocritical state of things, to prepossess the " conscience" in the law's favor.

But the horror with which the ignorant masses and weak-minded people were taught to behold a breach of the tube law will best appear from the following extract from one of their favorite poets :

> " The only way such guilt to cover,
> When on it glares the public eye,
> Is, for the beef and mutton-lover,
> To slink into some hole and die."

Although, as I have said, more than half the people were guilty of a breach of the tube law, and all would be if they dared, still, whenever one chanced to be caught in the act, the reproaches heaped upon " one more unfortunate" were unbounded, and always came thickest from those who sought thus to divert suspicion from their own guiltiness.

Parents, though themselves half-rotten with the shameful disease, abandoned their children, if the "misguided youths" became disgraced by, that is, surprised at, "free eating;" and public opinion justified stabbing or shooting those who helped others to "illicit" food, if the affair leaked out.

I saw an old and "highly respectable" man become incurably mad in consequence of his child having been caught eating an apple without having it half spoiled by the cooking necessarily preliminary to the nauseous process of sucking it through the lawful tube: for so destitute of a sense of justice had the tube law rendered the subjects of it that the disgrace of *discovened* illicit eating tainted every member of the delinquent's family.

Yet, strange to say, of every novel or play written, the breach of the tube law formed sometimes the tragic, but generally the comic part; and as if to show to what a depth they could sink in inconsistency, hypocrisy, and stupidity, the people, almost without exception, heartily relished a joke at the expense of the nevertheless cherished statute.

The tube law wss as murderously cruel as it was absurd and unnatural; for the obtaining of tubes depended, after all, greatly on tact, and even on chance; consequently, many of the simple-minded, timorous, and "law-abiding," died of starvation.

Tubes had also to be taken blindly, and retained exclusively for life, or whilst a vestige of them remained, however unfit they might be for use. Also, under certain circumstances, which very often occurred, they might be forfeited; when it became the duty of the forlorn individuals from whom they were taken, to live as long as they could without eating, and then die like good citizens, true to their "principles."

But need it be said that instead of so doing, most of these made it their chief business to seek out evasions of the tube-law, or to improve every chance of secretly transgressing it? A few however did not do so, and it was dreadful to behold those famishing wretches, those "martyrs to principle," in their agonies making the motions of eating—chewing the wind—till some of them, frantic, bit, often unconsciously, at whatever vile and even poisonous substances bore any resemblance to food; and they ground their teeth together and wagged their haggard jaws until they lost the power to do so, became maniacs, and died raving mad.

As a specimen of the senseless and absurd subtilties and impracticable abstractions, which this deluded people allowed themselves to be entangled in, and which they accepted for "law:"—The highest court decided that no one could be convicted of a breach of the "tube-law" on the strength of proof that the accused had vomited up food in chunks twice or three times as large as could have been taken into the stomach in the lawful way; nor was such proof allowed to be even offered in evidence. Neither could people be prosecuted or held to answer for a breach of the tube law in consequence of being more hale, stout and cheerful than they could possibly have become through the use of the tube. Even to express suspicions of such, was, by that most opaque and sophistical of possible entanglements which passed for "common law," decided to be libellous.

As new tubes worked better than old, clogged-up ones, there was a great temptation to destroy the latter; to do so was therefore, by statute, made the highest crime; which, on conviction, was punished by death. Corrosives were at first resorted to with great impunity, by those desirous of getting rid of their old tubes, and who understood the knack of immediately getting new ones; but chemical tests after a while put an end to the use of the coarsest of them. There remained one, however, and the most efficient of all, which, on account of its subtility, no chemical test could detect. Its use was mainly confined to the more refined and intelligent classes.

My pity was very much excited by the case of a poor innocent-looking young lady, who had not the tact requisite for the procuration of a tube, and who was consequently in the last stages of starvation.— Yet her own mother sternly refused her the use of food, declaring that she should go to her grave sooner than live disgraced by eating contrary to law; yet this same mother had "used up" no less than three tubes; was "working her card" for a fourth, and was, besides, in that robust and sprightly condition which could be accounted for only on the hypothesis of *sub rosa* " free eating."

A few were in favor of abolishing the tube. But these were opposed by those who led the multitude by the nasal organ, who asked : "If people are so gluttenous with the tube, and grow so big that charity often has to clothe and house them, what would become of them without it?" "Doubtless," admitted the few, "if tubes were suddenly abolished, people would, to make up for long deprivation, at first gormandise frightfully; since, throughout nature, action must have its corresponding reaction; but their unnatural or excessive appetites would gradually subside, after the withdrawal of the exciting cause; and then few or none would eat more than was necessary and proper; and, under a right condition of affairs, capable of being satisfactorily provided for.

But the tube law had been in vogue from time immemorial, and hence a sort of infernal charm seemed to sanctify it in the opinions of this besotted people.

Could they "set at naught the wisdom of ages, and consider their progenitors, who had tubed it so respectable through life as but a pack of fools?"

The tube law, by continually mortifying the appetite, soured the temper, and vitiated the feelings every way; and as parents transmit their bad qualities to their offspring, (and in a constantly more and more aggravated form, until the original cause of the evil is removed) drunkards, fools, lunatics, murderers, and miscreants of every grade, were actually begotten such; and the sticklers for the infernal tube carried their presumption so far (or rather, insanity so generally prevailed) that they accused "The Almighty" —(an immensely magnified photograph of themselves; including— of course—all their depravities) of thus "visiting the iniquities of the fathers upon the children."

At length, sickness from starvation so crowded the public hospitals, dead bodies so blocked up the streets, the "shameful disease became so general, and detected infringements of the tube law, so taxed the people for prisons and their keepers, that the said law thus rendered itself impossible to be enforced, and became a dead letter, wholly disregarded, either from motives of shame or fear; people grew up naked and homeless, from being too weak to furnish clothing and shelter for even their diminutive bodies.

What was to be done? Of course but one resource remained: the facility for the production of clothing and shelter must be increased. The public functionaries now took this view of the case, and in good earnest, set about testing its correctness, in spite of the warnings of sage old fogies who declared that nothing could be done except what already had been done, unless some way could be devised by which nature could be "*absolutely changed.*" The half naked, houseless wretches who mainly composed the community, and the capitalists and the skillful who, to some extent, in spite of all obstacles, still existed, now *organized* their combined force; an equitable arrangement for mutually co-operative *wholesale* productive purposes was made, and the best clothing, and the most magnificent shelter immediately became abundant, through mere necessary exercise on the part of operatives a little attention, by way of amusement, on the part of capitalists; and eating, to the full extent which nature required, and of course in utter disregard of the restrictive tube, became an honour instead of a disgrace; large people were emulated, and soon superseded altogether the half-dead wretches who, equally foolish, egotistic, and contemptible, had set themselves up for *facsimiles* of "The Almighty." Sickness, including even "the shameful disease," it is hardly necessary to add, soon became wholly unknown.

KING MULTITUDE'S CENSORSHIP OF THE PRESS.

Of all the subjects of King Multitude, editors and authors are the most abject, and most to be pitied. Under monarchy, editors and authors can calculate with tolerable certainty, how low they have got to bow—how circumscribed they have got to keep. But under multitudearchy, editors and authors, stoop they never so low,—cringe they never so small,—write they never so sycophantic or abjectly, they are never sure of not offending their dread sovereign. And if they please His Majesty to day, it's downright presumption to expect, *in the same way*, to please him to-morrow; for he is by far the most fickle sovereign that ever held sway, and incomparably the most expensive too. No nation ever endured him long at a time. No nation ever accepted him, without being so crazy that she had to be put into the straight jacket military despotism *right speedily*.

But King Multitude is a hydra headed oppressor, and it therefore sometimes happens, that he is so divided in his councils that a few authors and editors escape his vengeance, who write almost as boldly as they could under monarchy.

It is a ludicrous fact, that in writing the history of the revolution that gave King Multitude the American sceptre, the Hamlet of the piece—Thomas Paine—had to be left out, or barely alluded to, in order not to offend His Majesty. A fair History of that Revolution was written by Botta, *a subject of the Pope.* But when it came to be translated for the American Public, nearly all that related to Thomas Paine had to be expurgated. And this ridiculous Multitudearchy is christened *Liberty!* Well, *I take the risk* of saying that it's just the damdest humbug that ever was, or ever can be palmed off.

After all, the fault is not chargeable to King Multitude, but to the hypocritical, half-knave, half-fool, old fogey mystics, moralists, and demagogues, who lead His Majesty by the nose, and make him their tool and laughing stock. But they don't do this with impunity, though; their mock sovereign almost continually annoys them, and he sometimes turns on them like an infuriate tiger, or comes down upon them like a tornado, or a "thousand of brick."

Poor King Multitude! Your flatterers wheedle you into the position of both overseer and drudge, and all the other kings laugh at the absurd and ruinous blunders you make!

IS MONARCHY JEALOUS OF DEMA-GOGUERY?

European monarchs jealous of the "liberty" which caucus trickery and ballot-box jugglery bestow? Bah! Can such demagogue bunkum and clap-trap much longer befool and ensnare *anybody*? The monarchs of England and France have drawn their chief resources by means of what our cursed demagogues have palmed off on us for "free-trade," and free banking. Monarchs don't like to be stigmatized as tyrants by those whose *political* freedom is such a wretched patch-up of ignorance-spawned, nature-suppressing mysticism and "morality" which solely cause the abominableness of kings, that it has barely held together by means of flimsy cotton cords, and after a most woful, panic-stricken, sycophantic, corrupt, and bankrupt fashion eighty-four years, before hatching a tyrany throughout its southern part, that eclipses all the other tyranies that have ever existed—a tyrany that glories in theft of national magnitude, of property with which the thieves were entrusted, and which they voluntarily swore to protect! A tyrany that declares slavery not a temporary evil to be got rid of as soon as possible, but an absolute good, to be sacredly and eternally preserved, though civilization itself perish in its defence! A black slavery that is *now* the very bulwark of white slavery! The freedom of the system in which "Secession" could breed appears to me to be as *unreal* as the perfection of the "Heaven" wherein the "Devil" was spawned.

Demagogues! Instead of going to war to *enforce*

the "Monroe Doctrine," make our "freedom" a *reality*, instead of an *intolerable stink* in the nostrils of kings and their subjects. *That* will effectually and forever eliminate monarchy not only from America, but from the entire world.

THE NEW ERA.

Fellow Citizens of the United States! When the Secession war ends, we shall be compelled to pardon an amount of "criminality," compared to which, that of all the prisoners confined in our infernally cruel penitentiaries, vanishes into imperceptibility. Shall we also pardon those prisoners, and commence a policy that will forever prevent both wholesale and retail "criminality?" Or shall we imitate those poltroons who mistakenly pitch into rowdies as muscular as themselves, back out without punishing much, if any worse than they get punished, compromise with their offended dignity and prudent cowardice by thrashing the little boys who incontinently laugh at them, and ventilate their maliciousness by cowhiding their helpless wives and children *ad libitum* for imaginary offences? Shall we hang the perpetrator of *one* murder, and pardon, ay, fellowship with those whose hands are red with the slaughter of a million human beings? Shall we subject a poor wretch to long years of dreary torment, and to disfranchisement, for a five dollar property violation, yet receive into friendly citizenship those whose devastations, coupled with wholesale murder, have to be counted in billions, reckoning for Europe and America, and taking the damage inflicted on industry and trade into account? Let us put a final end to this system of punishing failure and rewarding success in villainy—to this abomination of abominations, which ignorance-engendered superstition's quintessence—" moral principle"—has palmed off on the world for law, and our praise and glory will be a universal chant, while earth and man endure. Let us celebrate our triumph over Secession in a grand universal forgiveness jubilee, and thenceforth set about placing mankind above the necessity or supposable necessity to err. *I have shown how.*

CHURCH AND STATE BLASPHEMY.

Governments as now constituted on " moral principle," are never long without being at war. Thousands are slaughtered to-day on one side, and thousands are slaughtered to-morrow on the other side, and both parties thank " God" for their victories.— Oh, how can beings with a particle of understanding suppose that any " God" except Moloch, considers himself honored by such thanks? Strange that the short-sighted multitude even do not see that these thanks are a most blasphemous subterfuge, under which priests and politicians hide their botchery. 'God' is the 'scape-goat' which carries the priests' and politicians' sins into the wilderness of " mystery," and the people stare and wonder, and don't see the trick of it. Church and State quacks never plunged a nation into calamity, whether of war or pestilence, that they did not exhort the people to " see the hand of God" in.

CONCLUSION.

Man will be actually and universally free, when *might really is right*; when power from its greatest to its smallest accumulation, is exerted as beneficially in the social as in the planetary system. Constituted by omnipotence, and assisted by the ablest exponents of *practical* law, *I have shown how all this will be accomplished.*

Rebellions closer and closer succeed rebellions. War has multiplied expensiveness till the whole world is bankrupted thereby. Prisons, alms-houses, and brothels, increase, oh! how fearfully; and State and City treasury stealing, oh! how astoundingly; witness what the State thieves and Common Council robbers, and army contractors, have done in the midst of our great national calamity! This horrible state of affairs cannot possibly go on much longer; it must crash under the weight of its own damnableness. The old world monarchs, the new world demagogues, and both religious and anti-religious moral principleists, must soon perceive that they are leading the helter-skelter rudimentary Social Organism, round and round in a hopeless Tantalia; in the very Utopia they so scornfully proclaim that they are opposed to.

And when they who lead mankind learn that to secure their own welfare, they must pursue a course totally different from the old one, "Secession" and every lesser abominableness will cease. *The* Union will " extend the area of freedom"—*real* freedom, *spontaneously*, till it encompasses the whole world;

right will, everywhere, take the place of wrong so easily, that everybody will wonder why the thing had not been done ages before. For self-interest, when rightly understood, will work as admirably as gravitation does, when we build, and operate in every respect, in accordance with a *thorough* knowledge of it. The mass of mankind follow leaders as inevitably as planets revolve around the sun. The body and head of the Social Organism will be as reciprocally, and harmoniously, and practically fitted to each other as are the Sun and his satelites; instead of being a " necessary evil," government will be a positive good, as beneficial to the body politic as the head of the perfect human being that is to be will be to his body. Nature will accomplish her grand aim at a blow, when all is ready. Ever since man's advent, nature has been faster and faster mustering her entire strength for the completement of "creation"—for the establishment of "Heaven" on Earth, and Nature is THE OMNIPOTENT, and cannot fail. All which has been demonstrated by the present writer, CALVIN BLANCHARD, announcer of *The Religion of Science;* professor of *Theo Religio Political Physics;* expositor of *The Statics and Dynamics of God Almighty.*

The Only Good Thing that can be done,

Is for France, England, the United States, or some other great nation, to enact a law emancipating love, and providing for the bringing up of all children so that they shall be perfectly healthy, perfectly beautiful, and perfectly good. Organizing labor, capital, and skill, so that there shall be no wretched creatures to fill up poor-houses, brothels, prisons, and standing armies.

The nation that first does this, will set an example that all the other nations will speedily follow, and her leaders will secure a universal gloria in excelsis whilst earth and man endure.

Anything short of this will be as vain, as would be an attempt to empty the North River into Long Island Sound, by means of pumping the former into the latter through an engine hose pipe, or forming societies for carrying the water across in junk bottles.

I appeal to the experience of ages for the truth of this!

Oh! ye mystical and moral betrayers of mankind! how much longer can you—even you—remain so blind as not to see this?

CALVIN BLANCHARD.

THE
WRITINGS
OF
CALVIN BLANCHARD.

IN 546 OCTAVO PAGES, $ 1.75; BY MAIL, $2.25.

I HAVE demonstrated that Nature is the All-Sufficient; that *She* "created" man, thus far, and must necessarily complete him, by creating all that his perfection, *as man*, requires.

Art is Nature's crowning method. By art, she produced the steam engine, electro-magnetic telegraph, and all the good that civilization contains more than savagery does.

Nature develops and reveals more and more rapidly, and her succeeding developments and revelations are more clear and important than the preceding ones. Thus, it cannot be long before she will convince the dullest of those who head the Social Organism, that by no possible devices can they secure their own welfare, at the expense of their fellow beings. This will introduce a system of law based wholly on physics, and calculated to fulfill, instead of *repressing*, human nature. This will put a final end to Church Atheism, State-Anarchy, and their fundamental ignorance built Utopia, and masked fountain of revenge, "moral principle." This will forever abolish the superstition-scourge, the monarchy-abomination, the caucus-and-ballot-box swindle or demagogue-pest, and the "duty"-compromise with wrong. This will so concentrate Nature's power, that she will sufficiently stimulate thermal and luminous action at the earth's poles, overcome tempests, volcanos, and too violent thermal action at the equator. This, and correlative arts, will transform the world to what the " Heaven"-idea glimmeringly presignifies. All labor that is repulsive will be done by machinery. Wealth and magnificence will be limited only by human wishes. All property will be held in *individual, interest paying shares*, by the Universal Mutual Guarantee Company. "The People" will dwell in palaces, splendid as the faith built "mansions in the skies." *All* the women will be enchantingly beautiful, all the men faultless, all the children will be so educated and provided for that they will be *real* angels. Love will be free and universally reciprocal, "virt e" and "vice" obsolete, all constraint banished, everybody completely happy. Between desire and its object, there will intervene only the exertion requisite to impart due pleasurableness to possession. Life will last till all clearly imaginable varieties of delight pall on the five senses from repetition. Sickness will be unknown. Death itself will be only a welcome, painless transit to everlasting forgetfulness.

All this is clearly preconceived, and therefore must necessarily take place. For thought is not absolute, but relative. The impossible, self-evidently cannot be conceived, even prospectively. Mentality does not transcend materiality, but functionally depends on it, objectively and subjectively.

The *true* function of government is to *annihilate* constraint; not to impose it. The " irrepressible conflict" is between the power that made THE CONSTITUTION of human nature, and the presumptuous, stone-blind parsons, politicians, and moralists, who persist in their miserable contrivances and worse and worse failing experiments for subverting that Constitution, and humbugging mankind into contentment with a mere fraction of the liberty to which that Constitution entitles them.

That prince of " devils," Ignorance, and that archdeceiver, Habit, have kept the world a vast Utopia— a double and twisted Utopia—a Utopia that so blinds its dupes that they look on evil as necessary and consider tantalism and failure as alone " practical." Let's put this new and all important question into colloquial form, and see if this is not the case :—

Question.—What is Utopia?

Answer.—A wild scheme; a plausible impracticalness; an alluring deceit; a tantalism; an undertaking of zeal without knowledge, sure to end in failure; in short, a humbug.

Q.—What is the most complete and shameful Utopia and failure, and the most impudent humbug that ever has been or can be?

A.—Moralism.

Q.—What is the next?

A.—Christianism.

Q.—How completely and shamefully has moralism failed?

A.—Moralism has been trying experiments on mankind ever since the beginning, with worse and worse results. Witness, the unprecedented and unsurpassable falsehood, corruption, injustice, cruelty, and *harlotry* that prevail in countries where moralism is in *highest* repute. With the exception of the present writer, all America goes for moralism; and only two solitary individuals (Fourier and Buckle) in all the world besides, have indicated their suspicions of its latent devilishness.

Q.—How completely and shamefully has Christianism failed ?

A.—Christianism far outdoes heathenism in spite, malice, and persistency in unsurpassable infernality. (*Vide* Secession, and England's atrocities in China and India.) Eighteen hundred and sixty-four years ago, according to the vulgar belief, Christianism proclaimed " peace on earth and good will to men ;" since when, there has been a rapid and most frightful increase of *war* on earth and the worst possible will to men. The most Christian as well as most moral nation in the world, also the richest, has, within three years, nearly exhausted its wealth and energies, and the wealth and energies of many unborn generations, in human butchery, and now the indications are that this butchery is not half through with yet; and this Christo-moral butchery has damaged all the other Christian, moral, and *civilized* (?) nations beyond all calculation ; and these nations have just gone in for a war that threatens to be yet *more* gigantic, bloody, and destructive.

Q.—What is the basis of moralism and Christianism ?

A.—Ignorance of natural law. Not knowing how to supply the demands of human nature, moralism and Christianism have undertaken to repress and smother them. In strict justice to the Christian doctors, however, it must be stated that they promise all who pay them money enough, *full* satisfaction *after death*.

Q.—What is the remedy for Christianism, moralism, and all other imposition, humbug, and evil?

A.—The Religion and Government of Physical Science and Art. The principles of this Religion and Government have created all the good which "civilization" contains more than savagery, although those principles have had to operate fragmentarily, and therefore under *all but* fatal disadvantages.

Q.—But why is it, that civilization is higher in Christian countries than anywhere else?

A.—That is *very* far from being the case in *all* Christian countries, but *true* civilization is *universally* highest where physical science and art have made the greatest progress. During the first fifteen Christian centuries, civilization was *much* higher in China and Japan than in *any* Christian country; it was fully as high, even in Mexico. Cortez, in his "*Letters to Charles V.*," acknowledged that Mexico was as well regulated as Venice—the *very* best regulated city in Christendom. The stories about human sacrifices in Mexico, prove to be little more than sheer fabrication, got up to justify Christian and moral robbery and murder.

Q.—How do Christianism and moralism unmistakably damn themselves?

A.—In sanctioning wrong and outrage so soon as these completely *triumph!* When insurrection, pillage, and murder "go it" strong enough to set up

Government, it is highly Christian and moral to obey, pray for, and sustain that Government!!!—Christian and moral laws professedly against murder and robbery, only punish those actively engaged therein, who don't "go it" on a respectably grand scale. Christianism and moralism are only a stinking rehash of rotten Paganism, which practically amounts to Atheism—to very Devilism. They apotheosize "necessary evil." They organize mankind into a mutual robbery and assassination club which shortens life by four fifths and degrades all labor to performance by whip-dreading Negroes or starvation-impelled white slaves.

Q.—Where are the principles of the Religion and Government of Physical Science and Art laid down ?

A.—In the *Writings of Calvin Blanchard.*

*   *   *   *

And now, ye parsons, politicians, and moralists, listen whilst I relate a true, and therefore to you most wonderful

VISION.

SCENE—A street in the largest city of the United States.

Enter a traveller from a fully developed planet.

Traveller—" Well, this is the best part of the world, they say. Yet things look most horrible, even here ; quite as bad as——"

Young America (sucking the stump of a cigar)—" Your'e a mighty handsome feller, by jingo! But what er yer grumbling about ? Ef yer don't like thes'ere deegens, why don't yer go where ye come from? Gut a king in *your* country, I s'poze ; gut 'em everywhere, except here. But this is a *free* country, sir; a *free* country, I'd just have yer to know."

Traveller—" What's the religion of this free country?

Young America—" Wy, the Crischun religion, uv course; it's ter du by others as we'd hev others du by us."

Traveller—" That's the same religion they have across the big water, where the kings are. They told me it was proclaimed about nineteen hundred years ago, as the religion of " peace on earth and good will to men." But almost the sole aim of its professors seemed to be—to cheat, impoverish, degrade, imprison, torture, stab, shoot, and hang each other. (Aside.) I wonder if it operates any better here?"

Enter a crowd of ragged Newsboys—" *Extree* Tribune! *extree* Times! *extree* Herald! Great news." (Traveller buys a paper and reads) " The bones of the Yankees, that bleach on the plains of Northern Virginia, if piled in a row, would make a macadamized road from Richmond to Washington." Twenty thousand Unionists burnt alive or torn to pieces by blood hounds! Fifty thousand secesh and forty thousand loyalists killed in the great battle! The black flag raised! No quarter on either side! Two million women and children starving to death in Dixie! Richmond taken! Six thousand prisoners blown sky high ' The rioters burning New York and trying to murder all black men, women, and children, together with those who would protect them. [Drops the paper in horror.]

"*That's* the way you do as you'd be done by, is it? *That's* the way your religion of "peace on earth and good will to men" works, after nearly two thousand years' trial; eh? I'm off."

Enter Calvin Blanchard—" Beautiful stranger, please accept this before you go." (Offering his " Writings.")

Traveller (opening the book) "What do I behold As I live, its the very system that prevails all over our perfectly happy planet!"

Moralists, Mysteryites, and Politicians! If you knew with what abhorrence you will be remembered in *the good time that is perfectly sure to come*, you would gladly barter your "immortality" even, for an exchange of places, on the record, with those you term the "vilest of the vile." But there is *one* way, and one *only*, whereby you can somewhat mitigate that abhorrence. Clothe yourselves in sack-cloth black as night, and nasty as the rag-picker can furnish. Down on your knees in the filthiest streets and lanes of the world's cities, bury your faces deep in the dust thereof, and implore the murderers, thieves, harlots, and beggars, who there inhabit, to pardon you. Acknowledge, in terms as supplicating and humble as possible, that your impostures and crimes are unsurpassable; that *your* guilt is the sum of *all* guilt; that you deserve " eternal damnation" infinitely more than do any other creatures who wear the human form. Beg hard on the score of ignorance. You can make a strong point there. In fact, *that's your only hope*.

Oh ye who most vehemently demand luxury and

magnificence, and every sense delight. My plan is ample. You can't desire more than it can give. It will prove sufficient for all mankind, forever. Once established, it will be as permanent as the order and mutual beneficialness that exists between the orbs, *both great and small*, which compose the Universe. *Actual and complete fulfillment of the constitution and laws manifested in human nature by the maker thereof.* THAT'S MY SYSTEM.

"Why don't the popular reviewers notice my book?"

I have not been so cruel and unreasonable as to present it to them. Galileo might as well have presented *his* great discovery to the Holy Inquisitors for a "puff." The reviewers (like the inquisitors) *might* be ever so well inclined, but what would that dread sovereign, King Multitude say to them, should they dare to *openly* differ with him in opinion? Just this:—"You can't get your living any longer by writing for me. Starve."

"Why don't King Multitude starve me?"

Because there are, even now, people enough who don't belong to his Majesty's oppressive gang, to sustain me in my undertaking; and the number and might of the latter are so rapidly increasing, that they must, before long, overcome the hellish influence which actuates the moralists, mysteryites, and politicians, and then we shall have *The Good Time.*

CALVIN BLANCHARD,
*Professor of Religio-Political Physics.
and Advocate of the Constitution
and Laws manifested in Human
Nature by the only possible " God"
—the really knowable Almighty.*

☞ *Something Peculiarly Rich.* ☜

SECRET HISTORY
OF THE
COURT OF CHARLES THE SECOND,
INCLUDING
THE AMOURS
OF THE
DUKE OF BUCKINGHAM
AND THE
EARL OF ROCHESTER.

The whole story exquisitely told, by the CHEVALIER COUNT GRAMMONT.

WITH A GAY FRONTISPIECE,

A very handsomely printed volume, of 342 pages, cloth gilt. Price $1 00. Postage, by mail, 15 cents.

THE ART
OF
REAL PLEASURE.
WITH A FINE STEEL ENGRAVING
OF
TITIAN'S VENUS,
AND
OTHER CHARMING PICTURES.

One handsome volume, cloth gilt, 85 cents. Postage, by mail, 15 cents.

THE ART OF REAL PLEASURE is the most sensuous book ever written. It's the great secret revealed, of *perfect gratification, without troublesome consequences.* It's just what every man and every woman wants.

Utopian Literature

AN ARNO PRESS/NEW YORK TIMES COLLECTION

Adams, Frederick Upham.
President John Smith; The Story of a Peaceful Revolution. 1897.

Bird, Arthur.
Looking Forward: A Dream of the United States of the Americas in 1999. 1899.

[Blanchard, Calvin.]
The Art of Real Pleasure. 1864.

Brinsmade, Herman Hine.
Utopia Achieved: A Novel of the Future. 1912.

Caryl, Charles W.
New Era. 1897.

Chavannes, Albert.
The Future Commonwealth. 1892.

Child, William Stanley.
The Legal Revolution of 1902. 1898.

Collens, T. Wharton.
Eden of Labor; or, The Christian Utopia. 1876.

Cowan, James.
Daybreak. A Romance of an Old World. 1896. 2nd ed.

Craig, Alexander.
Ionia; Land of Wise Men and Fair Women. 1898.

Daniel, Charles S.
AI: A Social Vision. 1892.

Devinne, Paul.
The Day of Prosperity: A Vision of the Century to Come. 1902.

Edson, Milan C.
Solaris Farm. 1900.

Fuller, Alvarado M.
A. D. 2000. 1890.

Geissler, Ludwig A.
Looking Beyond. 1891.

Hale, Edward Everett.
How They Lived in Hampton. 1888.

Hale, Edward Everett.
Sybaris and Other Homes. 1869.

Harris, W. S.
Life in a Thousand Worlds. 1905.

Henry, W. O.
Equitania. 1914.

Hicks, Granville, with Richard M. Bennett.
The First to Awaken. 1940.

Lewis, Arthur O., editor
American Utopias: Selected Short Fiction. 1790–1954.

McGrady, Thomas.
Beyond the Black Ocean. 1901.

Mendes H. Pereira.
Looking Ahead. 1899.

Michaelis, Richard.
Looking Further Forward. An Answer to
Looking Backward by Edward Bellamy. 1890.

Moore, David A.
The Age of Progress. 1856.

Noto, Cosimo.
The Ideal City. 1903.

Olerich, Henry.
A Cityless and Countryless World. 1893.

Parry, David M.
The Scarlet Empire. 1906.

Peck, Bradford.
The World a Department Store. 1900.

Reitmeister, Louis Aaron.
If Tomorrow Comes. 1934.

Roberts, J. W.
Looking Within. 1893.

Rosewater, Frank.
'96; A Romance of Utopia. 1894.

Satterlee, W. W.
Looking Backward and What I Saw. 2nd ed. 1890.

Schindler, Solomon.
Young West; A Sequel to Edward Bellamy's Celebrated Novel "Looking Backward." 1894.

Smith, Titus K.
Altruria. 1895.

Steere, C. A.
When Things Were Doing. 1908.

Taylor, William Alexander.
Intermere. 1901.

Thiusen, Ismar.
The Diothas, or, A Far Look Ahead. 1883.

Vinton, Arthur Dudley.
Looking Further Backward. 1890.

Wooldridge, C. W.
Perfecting the Earth. 1902.

Wright, Austin Tappan.
Islandia. 1942.

DATE DUE